Aaron Stevens Hayward

An Epitome of Spiritualism and Spirit Magnetism

Aaron Stevens Hayward

An Epitome of Spiritualism and Spirit Magnetism

ISBN/EAN: 9783337337186

Printed in Europe, USA, Canada, Australia, Japan

Cover: Foto ©Lupo / pixelio.de

More available books at **www.hansebooks.com**

AN

EPITOME OF SPIRITUALISM

AND

SPIRIT MAGNETISM;

THEIR VERITY, PRACTICABILITY, CONDITIONS AND LAWS.

BY THE AUTHOR OF "VITAL MAGNETIC CURE," "NATURE'S LAWS IN HUMAN LIFE," ETC.

BOSTON.
COLBY AND RICH, PUBLISHERS.
No. 9 MONTGOMERY PLACE.

PREFACE.

Our previous works having been favorably received, has induced us to continue to meet the demand of the times, therefore have written the following brief treatise upon two of the most important subjects connected with the life of human beings, trusting that the suggestions made therein will prove stepping stones to a better understanding of the subject, and will be the means of preventing souls from groping in ignorance and darkness in relation to the responsibilities and duties connected with human life in this world as well as in the spirit life.

Persons reading this book should for the time being lay aside prejudices and pre-conceived opinions, thereby becoming independent thinkers, being willing to receive truth for its own sake, accepting or rejecting whatever reason and judgment dictates.

Hoping this treatise may originate thought which will be profitable and worthy of the centennial year of this country, we send it on its mission of usefulness; and may it prove a blessing to many skeptical and doubting souls who would doubtless gladly receive the truth when fully demonstrated to their minds.

AN EPITOME OF SPIRITUALISM

AND SPIRIT MAGNETISM.

SPIRITUALISM is either a natural phenomenon or a myth—which? Does the spirit of man at "death" return to its original state, its individuality being annihilated, or is it an active, individualized personality in spirit life? Spiritualists are the only class of individuals claiming to know the fact and produce the proofs. Spiritualism, its use and abuse, its mission and ultimate, should be the great desire of mankind in this age of doubt, uncertainty and skepticism. Spiritualism, truth and facts, like honesty, are in many ways synonymous, all of them being unpopular; but when fully realized in their true sense, they will be appreciated and become the high standard for society to live and act by.

Realizing the necessity of a compact treatise, which explains the conditions and laws governing spiritualism and magnetism, the price to be within reach of all, we have endeavored to meet the demand; having obtained information that we consider would be beneficial to those investigating the subjects. We have designed the book as a missionary document, for the better understanding of the philosophy. We shall state facts obtained from personal experiences and investigations; also that which corroborates, selected from reliable individuals' testimony, leaving the readers to decide as to the rationality of the investigations, suggestions and conclusions.

The word "spirit" is printed in the Bible much oftener than any other word of note, thus showing it to be of great importance; in fact the value of the book lies in this word, when interpreted by the spiritualistic philosophy of the nineteenth century. There is no positive proof of immortality except by and through ancient and modern spiritualism.

"Covet earnestly the best spiritual gifts" was an injunction of the past. Why should it be ignored in this age by those claiming to believe that they existed in the past ages? Have the laws of life changed, or do individuals change their interpretation of them?

Spiritualism and magnetism having their basic foundation in laws, facts, truths and principles, they belong to all humanity; therefore must or should interest all mankind: these subjects cannot know sectarianism only as temporary in belief and action.

In the future with all mankind knowledge must take the place of faith and belief, in regard to the life in the beyond, (to many the unknown,) also will the material and spiritual laws that govern and control both spheres of existence be more fully realized and better understood.

It is worse than folly to attempt to force any particular belief upon mankind: anything that is known is far better than simply a belief in it. The public and world at large have had a false impression in regard to spiritualism, and its true mission and philosophy: they have the idea that it is with spiritualists imagination, illusion and delusion, more than reality; also that the future life is supernatural more than natural: these views must be eradicated before the mind can be disabused of such theories.

We shall speak our views and not another's, without they harmonize with ours: no one should be held responsible for another person's convictions and actions. We hold no one responsible for our views, let them be true or false, but shall express only sentiments that we feel to be truthful. We do not intend to advance speculative theories that will mystify the general reader, but on the contrary state facts and principles that will be realized as truths to many intelligent minds. We may not have discovered a new law or thought: there cannot be anything new in life forces, but they may be new and better understood by the masses, and become utilized and more practical.

We look upon the spirit world as the completion of earth life, the future home of all individualized intelligences in their varied and diversified conditions and development, each spirit gravitating to its own sphere, as growth will admit, and no faster; the locality of the spirit world being around and about the earth sphere, and holds a similar relation as do the material and spiritual bodies, or as the eye-lid does to the eye. Heaven we consider a condition of the spirit, instead of being in locality. Many persons get the two places confounded, and call the spirit world heaven.

Spiritualism to us signifies that spirits in both spheres of existence can visit one another, when proper and suitable conditions are complied with or obtained; also is a key to the past. Spirit power, vital magnetism and electricity are forces in nature without intelligence, which can be utilized and made beneficial in proportion as individuals understand them and know how to apply them, and no farther.

The conditions and laws governing the return of spirits are in perfect harmony with those of healing the sick by and through natural forces alluded to; therefore many things in relation to the one are to a certain extent applicable to the other, especially as far as conditions and the need of harmony. All forces in nature of necessity must work in perfect accord with nature's laws.

There cannot be anything miraculous about spirit return; such things must be a part of the great problem of human life, or else it only exists in imagination; it is the same with spirit healing; ignorance with regard to the laws of life may make the subjects appear miraculous to many.

Doubtless all sincere individuals desire truth in relation to the laws and conditions governing the spirit world; old forms, customs and beliefs have much to do with the existing prejudice concerning the spiritual philosophy, as understood by spiritualists.

Many persons believe as did their parents, not even presuming to question or think for themselves on the vital questions of the day; but take it for granted that belief insures eternal life, that is if that belief is in certain forms and dogmas; not even considering that their own individual opinions are as likely to be correct as the opinions of those who have preceded them, or those who are teaching doctrines that they never attempt to demonstrate, or give positive proofs of their truthfulness. We will not question individuals' honesty as to their religious views, when they are sincere; but as there are many who believe only with their lips, they being confirmed sectarian bigots, we desire to reach that class, and show them their inconsistencies.

Spiritualism is one thing; society and its actions are another: spiritualism has been held responsible, to a great extent, for the sayings and actions of individual spiritualists, which is entirely wrong. Spiritualism being a fixed fact, there is no more necessity of trying to prove it to the entire world's inhabitants faster than conditions and circumstances warrant, than there is to prove any other natural thing connected with human life and the universe, with this exception; of saving the human family from being led into false teachings, devoting time and money which might be expended in feeding, clothing and educating those who have been unfortunate. We would not ask individuals if their soul is saved, but try and discover if it is degraded, or if it has unfolded to the standard of its capacity, that it sees effects from causes.

Spiritualism has been accused of leading to dissipation. All that the public require to know concerning whether an individual is a spiritualist or not, is that he has been seen at a seance or a meeting where the philosophy is advocated: simply saying "I believe" does not make spiritualists, as it does sectarian church members.

The majority of individuals who have investigated the subject have made material application instead of the spiritual, attempting to a great extent, to make it turn to a mercenary purpose. Both spheres of life being essential, useful and natural, also closely allied; and as there are many things useful in earth life that are as dross in spirit life, therefore it should not be expected that the two spheres can work together in harmony, in the way of hoarding up material things. We have known persons whose sole aim seemed to be to gain material wealth, sacrificing the ordinary comforts of life, struggling and over-working their mental and physical system, for what in the last of their earth life they would have given their entire wealth to have had material life extended a few years longer: but Nature, true to law, said "No, your money will not buy it; you must go when disease gets an incurable hold of you." If spiritualism was applied to its legitimate use, it would command the respect of every reflecting, thinking person. Inquirers, skeptics, church members and even a large majority of spiritualists, in nine times out of ten, often consult spirits for the purpose of finding out something that relates to mundane spheres, more than to the spirit spheres. If individuals would consider for a moment, they would see great inconsistency in consulting spirits upon the trivial things that relate to every day earth life. If reliable spirits are in sympathy with our daily walks and actions, and they come to us with suggestions and advice, and we have confidence that their advice and judgment is superior to our own, then it is well to heed their counsel. The teachings that should be advanced are that each sphere of life has its own duties, work and adaptation; that both of them are in harmony with each other, when properly understood, is without question. The fault, if any, is with spiritualists and spirits, and not with the subject or law itself. Knowledge in the past was considered death and destruction; in the present it is life, health and happiness to all who are fortunate enough to obtain it.

To-day "spiritualism" and "magnetism" are household words in all parts of the world: those who oppose it, as a general thing, are those who know the least, or the whole subject from hearsay, having never investigated it personally, therefore their arguments are valueless compared with those who know the facts from personal experience and knowledge.

Some persons look upon the subjects as representing "evil," others as "good;" but notwithstanding all objections and obstacles that are brought to bear against them, they have become a vitalizing power in the world, and are receiving the attention of all classes of society, and of the most advanced minds in this and other countries; they having accepted the subjects as being truthful and the results of the universal law of life.

The new dispensation or spirit manifestations commenced some twenty seven years ago, in simplicity and obscurity, and has permeated all places; and to-day spiritualism is the progressive star of the nineteenth century. It seems well that its birth commenced outside of legalized creed, dogma and church organization, and that no religious denomination can own it, and thereby attempt to confine it to rules of their own making. The mission of spiritualism seems to be a leavening process more than a sectarian movement, and should not be set in hostile array in any other way than to undermine and diffuse itself amongst the entire human family. In England it originated or started in the higher walks of life, and is permeating all departments of human life as it is in this country, and is destined to become universally acknowledged by all mankind.

There are but few persons at the present time that think for themselves, but what acknowledge the existence of the different phenomena, but differ in their judgment as to the causes which produce the manifestations: some persons credit them to the author of all life; others accuse the "devil" with their authorship, and look upon him as not being included in all things. The latter conclusion is contrary to known law, and not in harmony with sound reason; therefore we shall endeavor to treat the subject on the broad universal platform, which includes the "devil" as part of the whole, the devil being simply undeveloped good, or a myth.

Our limitation of spiritualism is that it embraces all that exists; its platform is broad enough to include all mankind, and is as high, low and deep as the universe, and all contained therein; that it is connected with, and cannot be separated from all that exists. It solves the mystery connected with a future life, that has so long been a dark, doubtful abyss of uncertainties; and shows what the rewards and punishments are to be in case we disobey the laws of life, either physically, morally or spiritually. In fact spiritualism is a verity that is natural, and should not be questioned, as to thinking of changing the law that sustains it, any more than we should question the law that governs and controls the planetary system. We should accept all things in nature, and try to make them practical and useful. All things exist in nature of themselves from their own necessity, and are governed by natural laws. We cannot change the laws if we desire; they are beyond the control of finite mind.

Spirit tests and spirit identity are of such frequent occurrence that it seems futile to record them in this book: almost every family or some of their friends have received tests and experiences. There have been sufficient satisfactory facts and tests recorded or given to convince the entire world, if individuals could be convinced from the evidence of others. Personal experiences are the only realization and convincing proofs to many, of the truthfulness of the manifestations.

The law of *birth* into the spirit world is natural, and as essential as birth into the material world, and takes place alike with all human beings. All persons of intelligence acknowledge this fact.

We cannot see God and the universe in any other light than to be one great, grand, incomprehensible perpetual motion; self-sustaining, self-operating; the only one that can ever exist, that is without the finite can reach the full capacity of the infinite.

God in the constitution is the scheme devised by a few over-zealous individuals as a bolsterer and protection to sectarian religion. God cannot be seen alike by all mankind, neither can He be put in or kept out of the constitution. God needs no law made by man to protect or compel recognition. All shades of belief as to the great first cause—the source of all life, and the destiny of mankind are entertained by humanity.

The laws of life do not change, but individual opinions do. Our forefathers were not perfect, neither were their ancestors. To gain knowledge is not going backwards: the intelligent voters of this country are too far advanced in civilization to show in act what they cannot comprehend in knowledge. When our government attempts to force its subjects to accept dogmas, creeds and uncertainties as a religious obligation, then freedom—the true spirit of the constitution, will cease to exist. Intelligent persons must believe for themselves or they become slaves.

Human life, its origin, its unfoldment is to-day as well as in the past a mystery to mankind. But few pretend to connect the link in the chain of life, or to trace it back to its fountain head; but many there be that deal with facts and truths connected with human life, and from facts and principles discovered in life, obtained from the varied forms of investigation and development, give to the world the results of their researches and investigations. Such reports prove unsatisfactory to many individuals.

We cannot see that it is possible for the finite mind to ever reach out in full and be able to comprehend the infinite, except in a limited sense. Some persons may catch glimpses from a more exalted state, obtained from extended research, but still there seems to be more light needed to know all of life and its hidden mysteries in relation to mind, spirit and matter.

The higher or risen intelligences in answer to our questions in regard to the origin of man are as follows:

"Q.—If man is the highest development of known intelligent individuality existing in the earth-sphere, and is the result of time in development and unfoldment from the lower order of animals, and Nature's laws are immutable and unchangeable, why do we not see the unfolding process going on in this age as we do in all other lower forms of life in Nature?

A.—Nature ever has, and probably ever will, perform her works under cover, out of sight. The power that pushes matter on to its divine ultimate is an unseen power, a power that cannot be measured, cannot be weighed, cannot be analyzed. It is the Infinite, and because it is its manifestations are, in a great degree, incomprehensible. We see them when they are projected into outer life, but not before, never in any age.

This age is not behind any other age in showing its works of Nature, breathing out the revelations of the Divine; but on the contrary, is in the advance of all other ages.

Q.—After Nature has developed man through animal gradation, does the law cease to work in this form? And if so, does it not prove that the laws of life are changeable?

A.—The law never ceases to work, and yet its manifestations are infinitely changeable. The manifestation is the all of the law that you can ever know."

Salem witchcraft may have been premature or the "elementary" conditions of spiritualism, which time has developed into usefulness.

We know that we exist, and also that it was not our desire or wish that caused our existence: we find ourselves just as we are. We had no knowledge of life or individuality until we had remained in the earth sphere for several years, and come to growth sufficient to think and know for ourselves : identity is with us alike in degree. Idiosyncracies, disease and vices are to a large extent inheritances; individuals are not responsible for what belongs to generations preceding them : the well organized individuals should take no credit to themselves for being gifted or for having a healthy organism; but they can thank fortune and their parents for their fine inheritance. If persons are unfortunate in their inheritance they should try in all known ways to overcome, restrain and subdue vices, etc.

We cannot reconcile ourselves to the thought that we lived as an identity or an individualized spirit before birth into the material body we now inhabit. If it were possible for highly intelligent spirits to pass on to spirit life, return and take on the form of infants, what would be the necessity of their losing the knowledge gained in their first earth life? All children are compelled to learn first rudiments, let them be of high or low origin. Does the re-incarnation doctrine harmonize with any known law that can be satisfactorily demonstrated? The doctrine is either true or false. It would seem to us that a spirit like Daniel Webster would, when re-incarnated, be able to show marked scholarship in his second infancy, and save the necessity of primary school education in second and third infancy.

If the doctrine be true, why do we receive communications from spirits that have been acknowledged by its adherents to have been re-incarnated in other material forms, and are active in earth life. We think the doctrine itself needs no argument to prove its false premises : we cannot see human spirits to be omnipotent or omnipresent; or in other words, to be in two places at the same time. If they are in the spirit life active, they cannot be dwelling in human life as individual identities, as we see and comprehend life in the human.

Before entering fully into the subject perhaps an explanation, relating to why we remain or write incog. might be interesting to some persons: many have said "he must be ashamed of his works" etc. We will give a few of what seems to us satisfactory reasons; first, to deal with the subject independently of authority, that the readers may keep the subject constantly in their minds, instead of the author; also to avoid being personally criticised, instead of the manner in which the subject itself is explained. We are not ashamed of our views, neither are we of being known as author of the different works that we have caused to be issued, but feel satisfied that infallible authority should belong to the past instead of the present, which seems to us to have been a great hindrance in the march of progression thus far. We are also satisfied that principles, laws and their effects should be studied and dealt with, instead of individual personalities; that a greater good can be accomplished in working in this way than to have names more prominent than the subject treated upon.

We use the words *we* and *us* in preference to the pronoun *I* that we may avoid the appearance of being egotistical. We see daily where authority is worshipped instead of the truth itself; for instance when a "Rev.," "D. D.," "L. L. D." or some other title is used, or some renowned individual becomes convinced of the truths and facts connected with the spiritual philosophy, that which has been discovered by and through mediums, who have been teaching, through the aid of their spirit guides for the past twenty five years, and created a world wide interest; then it is that the renowned individuals will step upon the spiritual rostrum and advance the same teachings to old veteran spiritualists that have been recognized by all intelligent spiritualists until they have become a part of themselves. The new converts who have had but little experience, clothe their ideas in a little different language, and the public receive it because it comes from a noted individual; the same individual may have used all his or her energies until within a short time to prove the subject an illusion or delusion and fanatical in its tendency; but when the subject is presented by learned persons instead of by the poor despised mediums who have given the proofs of the beautiful philosophy, then it is that it is received by a large class of individuals, while the mediums are looked upon as stepping stones to convert the learned, and nothing more. Mediums are often placed aside to give place to new educated, converted skeptics, and inspirational speakers, that angels have educated for the work are often placed in the background, while those that have been educated in popular institutions (that must be broken away from before the truth can find utterance) are placed in the front. Some of our best inspirational speakers are forced from the field of labor from non-support, while learned individuals write lectures and read them in different parts of the country to full houses and at high prices; the lectures containing no new ideas, they having been advanced by mediums years previous, as the spirit giveth utterance, from the inspiration of the hour, then and there.

We are aware that there is danger of mediums becoming fanatical in their utterances, or psychologized and fascinated, but we also know that persons writing their lectures are not always correct in their statements, and often advance thoughts which soon have to be given up as being errors, opposed to the higher teachings as given by the advanced spirits in higher life. We do not desire to be understood as favoring ignorance to that of education, but we do know that philosophy that has benefited mankind came through the uneducated mediums, that the learned are forced to accept and promulgate; therefore we say let truth come, even if it does not stand the test of able criticism, as far as language and grammar are concerned. There are many mediums that have been truly martyrs to spiritualism, and have suffered for the material necessities of life. They seem to be moved upon to go and do things that seem inconsistent to many, and have been considered insane by those who have not investigated the different phases of spirit control.

Doubtless there are mediums susceptible to all kinds of baneful influences, embodied and disembodied, as well as those generated outside of individuality, which are produced by the inharmonious conditions and vices of society; such persons should be considered objects of sympathy and pity : but even spiritualists, that should know the laws of mediumship, blame such individuals for acts and sayings that the medium cannot resist or overcome; others set them up as teachers. We do not wish it understood that we advise individuals to follow fanatical teachings that originate from disorganized, undeveloped spirits, either in or out of the material body.

If persons are susceptible and are inharmonious, and have idiosyncracies, or are magnetically and psychologically attracted to undeveloped spirits or the spirits to them, and are influenced by such spirits, we, as intelligent human beings should have sufficient discernment to distinguish the difference between fanaticism and sound practical teachings.

If we find the intelligences that come to us are not practical in their teachings we should reject them, or not encourage them. We should not employ teachers or leaders who advocate teachings that are not consistent with advanced civilization: let them be controlled by either spirits in or out of the material form: we make no distinction between spirits in either spirit or earth spheres, without they are in reality of a higher type of intelligence and development. What is beneficial in one age may not be practical in the ages to follow.

We must not get false impressions into our minds and take the sayings of spirits through mediums just because they are spirits' sayings: in all cases we should judge of their truthfulness and reliability, and know for ourselves right from wrong; sifting the chaff from the wheat, accepting or rejecting all that our reason approves or disapproves; "believe not every spirit; try the spirits" is a good motto even if it is old.

MODERN INTERPRETATION OF THE BIBLE.

We find in reality that the Bible has no individual authority, and still it is not publicly questioned by the different church organizations. We look upon the record as simply history of the good, bad and indifferent acts of those living in that age; we cannot see wisdom in extending to posterity the record of some of the acts and sayings, which are said to have been performed and spoken by the so called "wise" and "good" men of the past; there does not seem to be any beneficial results following, that will be for the advancement of civilization; it may show the contrast between the lives of those living in that age and those in the present. But there may be serious objection to this, as many will have an excuse to practise or follow in the footsteps of their predecessors, and may be induced by reading the record to live the life that is said to be lived by some of the most noted men of that age. Where are the "Christians" living in this age, that will approve of the mode of life that Kings David and Solomon, also Judah and Lot lived in their social relations of life?

Also the killing of innocent children and women, leaving the beautiful young girls for base purposes, or of selling a fellow-being into bondage, and executing one of the purest and best examples of humanity, simply because he expressed his honest convictions as to what he considered to be justice and right. How can any person who uses his reason attempt to harmonize acts of individuals who (as the record states) lived in the past with those living in this age, except it be to show that what was wrong in the past must be the same in the present, and to disapprove of what we consider injurious, let it be either in the present age or in the past. The record states that the Lord put a lying spirit into the mouth of the prophet. Who believes such charges? No doubt lying spirits deceived in the past, as they are capable of doing in the present; but why accuse any one but the spirit itself of the act, or why should we ask the pure and good to "lead us not into temptation?" Would it not be better to ask such to prevent us from falling into it instead? How any intelligent individual can believe in the Adam and Eve narrative, except as a symbol, or the garden of Eden with its late hocus pocus interpretation, is more than the majority of spiritualists can imagine. The human organism being called the temple of the living God is well enough, and is nothing new, but we prefer to call the entire Universe the temple of the living God.

Was not John's birth prophesied, and did he not prophesy of Jesus' birth, and did not Jesus prophesy of others that would follow him? And why should we question the latter while the former was fulfilled?

Doubtless the most devoted worshippers of the Bible would not like to have many of its passages quoted in any other book, even if they are considered sacred in Bible history; if many of the statements therein recorded were expunged, the moral of the book would be enhanced and far more elevating to children who are compelled to read them; young children put to shame those of older growth, when in their simplicity, they question many of the sayings in the Scripture that they do not understand and which puzzles the "wise" ones to answer.

We do not consider the investigation of the Bible and giving opinions concerning it any more sacred or sacrelgious than it would be to investigate works on spiritualism, chemistry or astronomy. We take the Bible for what it is worth, but do not accept the sectarian church interpretation of it. Many individuals may say with their lips "I believe, God help my unbelief," but to us there seems to be a doubt of their full conviction, or their realization of its being anything more than a record of human origin, as all history is that is written in this age by human beings. We should take into consideration the forms, symbols and customs of the age, also the number of the inhabitants, section of country, and in thought and imagination go back to the time and consider the conditions and circumstances in which the book was compiled, and the reliability as to the authority, to be placed in its contents as a whole.

Deity being the author and finisher of all things, why should not his works be recognized in the history of the present age as well as in the past; and why in this new *era* or *dispensation* (which is as marked as any that preceded it) should there not be a continuation of what is known as religious history, one that will be an aid and benefit to generations yet unborn?

History cannot be confined or recorded in the past alone; therefore it seems to us to be consistent and advisable to have a continuation of history, or what might with propriety be called the second volume of the New Testament, which should be as reliable, and just as much from the author of all things as is the Old or New Testament. The different epochs of time should have their own records, and the present should harmonize with the past as fully as does the New Testament with the Old Testament. If this conclusion is not rational and natural, Oh! ye wise ones, please state why, and what are the objections to it.

Who are competent to compose a council, suitable to compile the work, thereby continuing on the history to completeness? Shall the work be compiled by sectarians, and be under military subjection, or be given to the most competent individuals who see and know the need of the history, and who may or may not be connected with the popular churches: competency and integrity seems to be the only requisite requirements needed in compiling the work.

We think this history must be obtained sooner or later, and individuals in different parts of the world are intuitively collating the needed material for the work.

The present Bible contains principally accounts of spirit manifestation, such as prophecies, visions, dreams and their interpretations, and a record of beneficial results from the use of spiritual gifts: also speaks of trances etc. precisely as are witnessed to-day, by those that will take the trouble or pleasure to investigate the laws of life. Who can say but what this age is as important as any that has preceded it?

To have a complete history of the spiritual work wherein the lives and acts of some of the martyrs and laborers in the present development of spirit power, those who oppose as well as its advocates should be recorded, seems to us to be the need of the times, and necessary for a completeness of spiritual history.

There is material sufficient to make a book much larger than either the Old or New Testament, but as all of it would be useless in history, it might be well to select what can be substantiated by the most reliable testimony, and reject as they did in the past, some individuals' testimony when compiling. Also to avoid giving several different persons' testimony on certain events, as was done in the past, let all the council agree upon what is to be recorded, and save the necessity of saying such and such persons make the statement: it should be the combined opinion of the council instead of one person's statement.

Why is it that there exists such a fear by the church members of investigating the truths and facts connected with the important subject of spiritualism is a serious question. Many persons dare not think for themselves; a false interpretation of past history has placed a fear upon honest, well meaning individuals.

The Roman Catholics, Second Adventists, Swedenborgians, Quakers, Shakers and Methodists have had what they call spiritual gifts. Other evangelical denominations have it in belief, but confined to the past instead of the present. The Methodists in their primitive days received and acknowledged spiritual gifts, more than they do in their present prosperous condition. Formerly they encouraged the exercise of them when they appeared; in the present they reject the power and gifts; for instance some of their members at a late camp meeting were influenced; they were ordered to stop such proceedings on the ground. At another meeting a member was entranced for a long time, by what they termed "slaying power." He was like a dead man, but the society refused to give credit to its being the same kind of influence that was prominent with them in the past, or that is so common among the spiritualists, and without question the same as came upon St. Paul, St. Peter and others in the past.

Inconsistencies abound with the different religious teachers. When will individuals have the moral courage to think for themselves? We consider a Methodist meeting where there is a oneness of spirit, a willingness to receive, and harmony abounds, which is created by the psychological power of some psychologist preacher (what is termed by some a revivalist,) or by singing, the best conditions that can be obtained for a seance: spirits can gain possession of sensitives better in such conditions than they can in a seance that is held where there are as many different opinions as to conditions requisite, as there are persons attending it. Spirits return by a natural law, the same as they leave for the spirit life; and it matters not whether they are recognized or not, the *fact* is the same, but the results are not as favorable for the spirits to make themselves recognized; but as far as conditions for gaining control are concerned in harmonious gatherings, they cannot be excelled.

Spiritualists at this time should know full well that contention, different opinions, "side issues," that cannot be seen alike by either spirits in or out of the material body are obstacles to healthy growth and unfoldment of spiritual gifts, which should be considered when manifestations are desired.

Seances composed of promiscuous persons, also inharmonious public meetings are neither beneficial to society nor sensitives, and should be avoided as much as possible by all who are in a negative state. When antagonistic, opposing influences are brought to bear upon sensitive organisms, it often proves detrimental in many ways, therefore this word of caution. A natural, steady growth is the most practical in development; also an interior unfoldment first, then the external, thereby becoming assisted by spirits while individuality is retained.

Mediums generally are obliged to come to this condition sooner or later, if they prove useful in the field of labor. There are but few exceptions to this rule, either in the past or present, that we have discovered in mediumistic development. The spirit world is inhabited by all classes and all grades of spirits, once dwellers on the earth sphere; without question there are many mediums as well as individuals deceived by designing, "seducing spirits," who take delight in creating inharmony in all departments of human life. Some of the sensitives are willing instruments in their power. We cannot see any other solution to the subject that reason sanctions: this must be a natural consequence, judging from this sphere of life.

When individuals understand that every act in life, good or bad makes the man or woman, and that mean low acts cannot be forgiven, except by growth and by overcoming evil with good, then will they do right for their sake as well as that of humanity. Spirits are attracted to those on earth that will cater to their mode of life, or a life similar to that which they lived while in earth sphere, let it be good or its opposite. Spirits gain control of individuals by a natural law, they differing in growth and desires as are the characteristics prominent in the spirit seeking control; the effects and results of its mission depending upon the spirit itself, and not the law or the fact. They may come for selfish indulgence in vice, for pleasures or for the elevation of humanity; just the same as do spirits living in human bodies to-day, acting from their own peculiar development.

MEDIUMSHIP; ITS LAWS, AND THE RELIABILITY OF SPIRIT COMMUNICATIONS.

The word medium has many meanings, but when connected with the spiritual philosophy it means that certain individuals are susceptible to the influences from disembodied intelligences, also are susceptible to positive spirits living in this sphere of life. Most persons are more or less mediumistic and susceptible to spirit influence or control: whether acknowledged or not, the fact is the same. Spirits in the mundane sphere affect individuals pleasantly or otherwise by daily interchange of thoughts: even when both agree, the effect is the same in many cases, which we claim is caused by the life forces generated in the different organisms, or the influences attracted to them being either harmonious or antagonistic. There is as much diversity in the effects produced upon different persons as there are differences in temperament and susceptibility; many have full control of themselves, while the spirit leaves the impression upon the brain or controls their hand either mechanically, or impreses them to write what is imparted first to the brain.

With some mediums the spirit gains full possession, the mediums remaining unconscious, not knowing one word that has been spoken through their lips. This phase of mediumship would be the means of convincing the most skeptical: many think this control the most reliable, therefore the best, which might be the case, if we could always be sure that a reliable spirit is in possession of the medium, or if it was sure that it is the one that it claims to be; but as there is such deception practised both by spirits in and out of the body material, it stands us in hand to be on guard: persons are full as liable to be deceived by spirits out of the material form as in, therefore we consider it wisdom to state facts as they are, that the investigator and skeptic may know just how much reliability the spiritualists place upon the teachings of spirits.

Without question the spirits are as truthful to-day as a whole, as they were in the past ages: many of the prophecies made in the past, as those in the present, are truthful and have been fulfilled; others would not have been fulfilled if it had not been for the persons having them made to, felt it a duty in some cases to carry them out, "that the prophecy might be fulfilled" as was spoken by the prophet: for instance in the past, the case of Jesus, when on arriving at the gate of the city, he was obliged, as the record states, to send for the beast that he might ride into the city, as was prophesied.

We will relate two cases of clear seeing or prophecy, that we are personally knowing to the facts, and which can be vouched for by the persons receiving them.

A lady medium said to one of the principal merchants of Chicago a few years ago, "The boiler of your engine at your store is unsafe." By examination it was discovered that a spot several inches square had become worn so thin that it was transparent, and was liable to burst at any hour. The timely warning no doubt saved an accident. The same lady met Mr. Hartshorn, an engineer on the Old Colony railroad, the evening before the sad gas explosion on the South Boston bridge; she said to him "You have a friend (not in your family) who will soon pass to spirit life suddenly; you will be greatly surprised on hearing of his death." In less than twenty four hours Mr. Sanderson was numbered with the victims of the explosion. Mr. H. says he never was more surprised than when he heard of his sad fate, and then flashed the words upon his mind that had been spoken by the medium. Generally he and this friend took the same horse car to go to their business, and greeted each other mornings with "How are you, Chummy?" Whether the sad fate could have been averted if Mr. H. had questioned the intelligence in relation to the friend will never be known: not being a spiritualist, he neglected to question concerning the friend. In both of the above cases the medium was an entire stranger to the parties, but to-day they will corroborate the above statement.

We consider the communications no more reliable or truthful, or to be received any sooner than they should be if they came from the same spirit provided it was an inhabitant of the mundane sphere; that is without the spirit has been in spirit life a sufficient time to have gained more knowledge and wisdom than it possessed before it reached spirit life: there are many sanguine spirits in spirit life, as well as in this life: they may come to us with all assurances imaginable and make statements which may or may not prove true: they are as liable to err in judgment as they did while in mundane spheres of life. We make these statements for the benefit of those who have had but little experience and who think that nothing but truth and perfection can emanate from spirit life.

Our experience goes to prove that spirits are no more

perfect in one sphere than in the other; they are in both spheres capable of growing to a higher state of perfection.

In prophecy, much depends upon the medium as to its reliability or of its being verified; many spirits are willing to give their opinion concerning future events, which should not be taken as prophecy or as being infallible any more than if they were spoken by the same class of spirits in this life. It is often more in having good judgment than the gift of prophecy, that spirits in both spheres get at facts and truths. We consider that mediums are unfolded in some cases to prophesy or to see future events, but the majority of the mediums in the present time are exercised for spirits to manifest themselves, which is for a different purpose than for prophesying. Mediums themselves are often deceived by spirits, saying and doing things that are not truly honest, at times being under the control of mischievous spirits. We should in all cases know whether the spirit controlling is guilty or whether the medium is practising deception. In some cases it is difficult to state for a certainty, therefore caution should be exercised where there is a doubt; but where it is once fully known that the medium is guilty of practising deception under the guise of spirit manifestation, spiritualists should discountenance their doings, even if it does have a tendency to destroy public confidence in spirit manifestations. Doubtless some mediums pretend to be unconscious when controlled, when in fact they are not, and by this way gain knowledge of their sitters' secrets.

If a spirit does not have a clear knowledge of our wants, conditions and circumstances without being told, it may be set down as almost a certainty that it is not our spirit friend that is answering our questions. Spirits to give valuable advice, must be knowing to the wants and circumstances of the individual. There are too many mediums that are like machines, and want the investigator to ask questions that can be answered by spirits in the form as well as out, by "yes" or "no," which are as likely to be false as true. We have long since discovered that it is not profitable to question a spirit without said spirit shows that he knows us without an introduction. There are persons who go to mediums and expose their entire business: an unprincipled, smart medium or spirit could answer almost any question; but the most important thing is is to be led or counselled in the right.

An individual abounding in material force, styling himself a detective medium commenced to expose mediums, calling the whole spiritual phenomena a delusion and the mediums humbugs, and after travelling the country over as an "exposer" he found that an invisible power at times would take possession of his organism, and that manifestations were done through him that were beyond his own physical action and knowledge. On this discovery, in giving public seances he did not pretend that they were or were not done by spirits, but let the audience decide for themselves whether he was assisted by spirits or not. In this way, he said he could draw not only spiritualists but skeptics, and thereby reap a great harvest; at the same time avoid giving free tickets to spiritualist societies. He also says his aim and object was purely making money: the world owed him a living, and it was no worse for him to cater to the public credulity than it is for ministers and men engaged in other professions. He had in his employ a minister's son, who is naturally gifted and understands the ways of the world, and can talk the spiritual laws with much ability and truthfulness; but after he gets through with his lecture he is often found following the Bible injunction in taking a little wine for the stomach's sake; and in this way the spiritualists are ashamed of his acts, and the skeptic cannot see anything good in spiritualism. The example is bad, and far from being spiritual in the true sense. This medium in private conversation acknowledges that he is a full believer in the spiritualistic doctrine, and gives for an excuse for deception at times the following reasons; first, he has to spend much time and expense in securing a hall, also in advertising, and is not sure of the first manifestation, but his expenses for license etc. must be paid, and when he has a full house and the spirits do not come to his assistance, he makes up bungling manifestations and gives something at random as "tests;" these not being satisfactory to the audience, being detected in the deception, they pronounce him a fraud; and he goes to another town and perhaps better conditions are given the spirits to manifest, and then he comes off victorious, and so goes from town to city all over the country, coining money from citizens with different religious beliefs. He says he avoids sensation and positive persons, as such destroy the conditions for the spirit control: he can tell when the power is upon him, and can do nothing satisfactory without it, but he must deceive when it is not upon him, for the purpose of keeping the money taken at the door. He says he shall continue to do so until audiences understand that he has nothing to do with the *genuine* manifestations, and they are willing to pay him for seances whether they obtain manifestations or not. We can see much logic in his argument upon the material, money making plane of life, but not the first particle from the true spiritual stand-point. Without doubt he is attracting attention to the subject. His agent may have been born with hereditary inclinations for strong drink, which can be looked upon as a great misfortune, and his actions not worthy of the cause he is engaged in, but still it does not prove anything against the phenomenon being a fact, but may retard its progress for a season. Are such proceedings of more benefit than injury to the cause? This medium makes an open confession that he cheats at times, and states publicly that he does not believe that there is a genuine physical medium before the public but what at times palms off bogus manifestations for the genuine ones. We are satisfied that he is mistaken, and that he is practising to-day what will in the future look to him as being far from the better way, and when he becomes spiritualized he will see from a different stand-point. Often persons question sensitive mediums in relation to the reliability of their communications, in case they should have a seance with them. Doubtless such questions and lack of confidence destroys the harmony and will be the means of not getting satisfactory communications. Mediums should not be disturbed in any form before a seance, but speak "as the spirit giveth utterance," trusting the spirit to give whatever is best, or needed in each individual case.

There are many honest, sensitive mediums who will not allow their organisms to be controlled by promiscous spirits: some of them can ward off the control, others cannot; therefore many times there is danger of sensitives being controlled by undeveloped spirits, especially when they have no one that possesses the positive will force to assist them in warding them off.

Mediums are often degraded by spirits of low, vicious propensities; we call such control a species of obsession, or incarnation; in fact all spirit control can be called possession, the control differing in degree as the spirits differ, in their understanding and goodness.

Bible history states that wicked spirits were attracted to some individuals, and the last state of the persons was worse than the first: what is this but retrogression for the time being?

RE-INCARNATION.

The following is a species of re-incarnation; spirits having had control of progressive mediumistic individuals in all ages; impressing them to say and to do many things beyond what they knew or the age they lived; when such persons are born to spirit life, their controlling guide may or may not continue in spirit life with them as guides, but our investigation thus far goes to sustain the theory, that on entering spirit life, the guides find some other mediumistic individual living in earth life, just the same as do the mediums themselves when they return to friends. In this solution it shows that the spirit of mediums that have not grown to the capacity or understanding of their controlling guides will on returning to earth show that they are not as well informed as they were while living in the material body, with the aid of the knowledge obtained from the controlling guides. This explanation may solve the question that is often asked, which is this; "Why do spirits not show as much ability after the change 'death' as they did before?"

Well informed spiritualists are not afraid that their beautiful philosophy will be destroyed, but prefer to state facts as they find them, that the public may know the whole truth as it is, as far as they are able to discover it. It is far better for all persons that the subject should be presented in all its diversified bearings, and the rocks and quicksand (if any) be shown; thereby saving individuals from temporary disappointment; this is the reason that we state facts, that skeptics and investigators may not feel disappointed if they do not get proofs satisfactory in an hour or in years.

There are many things connected with the spiritual philosophy that seem almost incredible; but are vouched for by creditable witnesses, as being genuine manifestations of spirit power: they are almost equal to the fish and quail stories related in the past history.

Spiritualists themselves cannot explain by any known law some of the seeming mysteries connected with the philosophy; time may develop a solution of them, as far as it is in the power of the finite mind to comprehend the infinite. There seems to be a wide difference of opinion amongst its advocates concerning the manifestations; this may be the design of the higher intelligences, which prevents sectarian organization amongst them, and do away with idol worship.

It takes a life-time to know all that there is to be learned in this philosophy: it is no superficial thing that can be learned from books alone or from institutions; but it is individual growth and experience that settles conviction in the minds of all thinking persons.

There are many individuals who on becoming convinced of the reality of spiritualism abandon their legitimate occupation at the suggestion of some impractical or perhaps some mischievious spirit. Individuals do not seem benefited when they are constantly soliciting aid from the spirit life to do their material work for them: each sphere of life has its own work; both can be in harmony, but the conditions for spirits out of the material form are not as natural to perform material labor as are those in mundane spheres, as we understand it.

The majority of those consulting spirits do so upon the mundane plane of life, and upon things that they should be better judges of themselves; therefore dissatisfaction and inharmony are the results in many cases.

A martyr to principles seldom gains or desires worldly riches. What was done by a martyr in the past, and whose life was held up as an example, also is worshipped to-day by persons who consider the acts he committed to be criminal and punishable, if practised in this age by any other individual. Doubtless in the great future all persons will be weighed in the balance of equal justice, motive and growth being considered in each individual case, without regard to the forms and customs of the age in which they lived.

Some spirits now as in the past take no thought concerning material things, at times leading their subjects from place to place, not allowing them to accumulate material things, or even possess sufficient to obtain the necessities of human wants. How can such conditions be looked upon as being advisable when the individuals that assist those who are destitute are prosperous, and they look upon the persons thus led as unfortunates instead of true practical missionaries in a useful work? "The laborer is worthy of his hire," but in most cases the persons led show no practical work, not even having the power to convince the public of spirit communion, or of its being worth obtaining. We feel sorry to make these confessions, but do so as a duty, that the public may know what spiritualists look upon as practical and what is the reverse, which takes the form of fanaticism.

Without question much that passes for spirit control partakes largely of the mediums; for instance the medium while in sympathy with an individual, gives satisfactory communications, but when anything offends the medium the "spirit" control changes, and instead of bestowing favors as formerly, it traduces. This shows conclusively that the mediums are not under the control of the higher intelligences, also that they are on the selfish plane of development, or not controlled by spirits at all. Investigators should learn that the same universal rule should be applied to spirits living in both spheres of life: doubtless both spheres of existence contain selfish spirits. We could relate some absurd, ridiculous examples where spirits through mediums have suggested favors being bestowed where they were not worthy of them.

We could cite thousands of valuable, useful as well as reliable communications, but as they are so common and almost in every family, we will not allude to the truthful ones, but will speak of a class that do not prove reliable and trust-worthy, therefore cause much misunderstanding. Spiritualists do not claim perfection in spirit communications. The *Banner of Light*, a weekly paper devoted to the promulgation of the subject, has at the head of its columns the following words, which shows the estimation placed upon them by the oldest spiritual paper now before the public.

"Each Message we claim was spoken by the Spirit whose name it bears through the instrumentality of

MRS. J. H. CONANT,

while in an abnormal condition called the trance. These Messages indicate that spirits carry with them the characteristics of their earth life to that beyond—whether for good or evil. But those who leave the earth sphere in an undeveloped state, eventually progress into a higher condition.

We ask the reader to receive no doctrine put forth by spirits in these columns that does not comport with his or her reason. All express as much of truth as they perceive—no more."

Spirit communications are no doubt tinctured more or less with the mediums. The intellectual, moral and religious elements have but little to do with the physical manifestations. The adapted chemical forces of the medium seem to be the essential elements required: there does not seem to be any fixed standard for spiritualists; each one acts from his or her individual stand-point, or else they are hypocrites. In fact no person can go above or below their interior growth, and remain long. The more spiritually, intellectually and morally unfolded the person is, the nearer they arrive to the high standard of perfection, Deity.

We will give our experience as to the reliability of spirit communications in certain cases which have come under our personal observation. Not long since we advised a friend to visit a test medium of note, who gave him undoubted proofs of the identity of his father's spirit: he was more than delighted, was perfectly satisfied of its being what it purported to be, but being of a worldly turn of mind his first thought was to question him on money making. The spirit seemed to understand the question and gave advice which was heeded and carried out, proving unreliable or a failure, making a loss of considerable money. This made my friend more skeptical than before he investigated the subject; therefore rejected it in full. He knew that his father would not have advised him so foolishly, he being a spirit of sound judgment while in the body. Without question some spirit was attracted to him who represented his father's spirit and gave wrong information, just the same as is practised daily in mundane spheres by strangers representing themselves falsely.

Another case with another medium. A gentleman consulted a prophetic medium concerning his wife's health: the encouragement given him induced him to consult another; this one gave many things like the first, afterwards made a prophecy which was entirely different from that of the first: both were positive in their assertions, and doubtless were made to state what they did by a power foreign to themselves. We heard the husband relate the messages to his wife, and we could not help thinking how incorrect the statements were from the true state of things. It was soon ascertained that both were false in their assertions or prophecy.

There may be wisdom in not informing patients of their near approach to the better life, as was done in the last case. In many cases we have known spirits through mediums to make a prophecy to persons concerning their death ; the effect upon the individuals was depressing, and no doubt detrimental. For instance some persons as in Bible times are symbolically controlled, seeing all kinds of animals, snakes, coffins, daggers, death and destruction, even when it does not in reality exist, not even in spirit. In one case some fifteen years have elapsed since the prophecy of death, the individuals being to-day in far better health than when the spirit uttered the words. The symbols might have been intended to be entirely spiritual and were interpreted materially, but the effect seems to be injurious and unwise, judging from the mundane stand-point.

There are spirits that seldom give any persons communications except in flattery ; others will not be bought or sold, but give things as they see them without fear or favor. Mediums prosper best materially when they attract a class of spirits who are "all things to all men," but such will not endure except it be for a season. Judicious spirits never expose the faults of their friends to other persons, except it be to benefit, but often reveal them to individuals to reform them.

Mediums are not at all responsible for what is imparted by the spirits through their organism ; it only shows that communications from disembodied spirits are like those from mortals, therefore reason and judgment should be exercised in proving their reliability and truthfulness. Investigators and skeptics who are honest in their investigation should not be condemned at wholesale for not seeing things through believers' eyes. There is more harm in believing too much without proof than there is in not enough. Mediums partially unfolded, or if they are controlled by unreliable spirits, placing themselves before the public, advertising for patronage, must expect to be criticised and tested to the extreme; and if they are not in a condition to overcome such obstacles and skepticism, they should avoid placing themselves before the public in the capacity of paying, public mediums, except with provisos.

We will give a few more items of unreliability in communications that the subject may be shown in all its bearings. A person had an intimate friend living at a distance who was quite sick; a spirit through a medium said that she could be cured, also stated how it could be done. The person on returning home found a letter which contained the sad news of the friend, she being an inhabitant of spirit life, while the spirit was giving the information that would restore her to health. The conflicting words made the skeptical inquirer more doubtful than before as to the reliability of spirit return.

What one person accepts as a test, others account for in a natural manner, without the aid of spirits. A person called on a medium and received what he considered a reliable and satisfactory seance: the individual told the medium where he was from, and that it was the only time that he should have for a seance, as he was to leave the city soon. The medium under "spirit control" said "You are going to ——," naming the place; "No," said the person, such a place, giving the name. "Oh! yes" said the spirit, "that is it"; and then goes on and says you must do so and so on your arrival. We can see no test in the above, but the individual was perfectly satisfied. Many drink in all that is stated to them by spirits through a medium, not stopping to question.

In the last case alluded to, the medium may not be at fault, therefore they should not be sensitive when such things are made known for the benefit of the public and cause.

From curiosity and to test a medium an acquaintance took a lock of false hair from his worn-out top piece, and forwarded it by mail to a noted medium or psychometrist. The answer was returned, stating that the person had a tape worm; a recipe for medicine was sent that would extricate it. The answer may be correct, or it it may not: it would be difficult to state for a certainty whether the person who had the hair cut from his head (that the top piece was made from) had a tape worm or not, but it was considered by the skeptic a failure, the medium a fraud or humbug. If deception had not been sent to the psychometrist, better results might have been obtained. If we expect and desire honesty and truth, we should not bait our questions with deception and falsehood.

We know of persons who have visited mediums for the sole purpose of finding out when their partners were to take exit to spirit life: invariably did the answer come in echo according to their own spirit desire, the spirit stating that at such a time the link binding the spirit to the material would be broken. The consultations were kept up with different mediums for years, and to-day the partner is in better health to all appearance than at the time of consulting, some twelve years ago. This shows that some spirits cater to the morbid imagination or desire of individuals, therefore should not be sought for any such purpose.

A public medium named her canary bird after an eccentric woman. She soon sickened and report said was near death. This medium prophesied that the death change had come to the woman, as the bird had died. No doubt there was more sympathy than mediumship in this prophecy. Another medium prophesied that a noted spiritualist who was returning from a long absence, on board of a steamer, had been shipwrecked and never would reach the shore alive. He was willing that the truthfulness of his gift should be judged by the future results of his prophecy. In both of the cases named there was no truth in the statements made. This shows that we should not place implicit faith in all that is given by and through mediums, and that as of old there are spirits of all grades of truthfulness on the other side, as there are in this sphere of life; therefore no infallibility will be recognized by well informed spiritualists, even if church members hold that such a state exists outside of the infinite.

We do not wish to be understood as ignoring the gift of prophecy, but think it most reliable when it comes unasked. Without question selfish spirits who work on both sides of questions, give advice on marriage as well as on other questions, which prove no more reliable than if it were given by the same class of spirits dwelling in mundane spheres. Marriage consummated under such spirits' advice, in nine times out of ten does not prove harmonious or beneficial. We should know the counsels to be reliable before acting upon their advice. There are some highly sensitive mediums who have a feeling of repulsion of being a receptacle for all classes of spirits, therefore will not be influenced except under certain conditions, and when with persons that are beyond reproach, they do not seem willing to meet the conditions that are often required by skeptics. Some mediums can give reliable communications to one person to-day and not tomorrow, while with others they cannot give anything that is satisfactory; such things are accounted for, when individuals understand the governing natural law that spirits employ.

There is no question but what mediums have "familiar spirits" as is spoken of in the Bible, who act for the spirits of friends at times as messengers, and can read questions in the minds of others, and answer them from their own stand-point; the questioners seeing that the questions are understood and answered, take it for granted that their spirit friends must have been present to have known what the question was; but if they would consider for a moment they must know that one spirit as well as another can read thoughts and answer mental questions. The questions may not be as satisfactorily answered by one spirit as by another, but still they are answered, and we make these suggestions not to disapprove, but more to get at facts, truth and the foundation of the subject.

Doubtless mediums for gain are knowingly and willingly influenced by spirits to take both sides of a subject or question, and will assist in consummating a scheme, trade or plot where one of the parties will be benefited at the expense and injury of the other, just the same as is practised in mundane spheres.

We have known cases of this kind, where the medium knew from actual knowledge both sides of a trade, lawsuit, also a divorce suit, and the medium kept both parties in ignorance of anything being known, except what was claimed to be given by spirits. Such acts are anything but honest, and should not be countenanced by spiritualists.

Where mediums and spirits can work for both parties for simply justice to the right, it should be encouraged and commended; but as there are many selfish spirits in both spheres of existence, and with many might makes right, therefore we should be cautious in taking the advice given by different spirits, as we may be receiving advice that may not be for our best good. Mediums, ministers and politicians without principle at stake, who stoop to gain popular favor by selling themselves for simply gain should be placed in the same category; policy has been indulged in too frequently for the best interest of society. One of the most detrimental things in spiritualism is that mediums are flattered and puffed up at times, and are taking high prices for seances while other mediums who are equally as worthy, but having no personal ability or shrewd financial agent to put them before the public, are working night and day in the cause for a small pittance.

The philosophy of spiritualism is not injured by this solution or explanation, but on the contrary is made more reasonable and satisfactory, as we understand it. A spirit having the power to return from the spirit life settles the question with all rational, reasonable persons. Making *practical* the knowledge obtained is, or should be the work of to-day, therefore spirits and mediums should be willing to be tested in all ways best suited for the true, honest investigator. Individuals should give mediums and spirits all suitable, honest means to accomplish their mission.

Well informed spiritualists look upon the spirit world as they do upon earth life, as far as being inhabited by different grades of spirits, differing in degree both in mentality and knowledge, also moral development; each living in their own individual sphere, the information received from them to be as reliable and no more so than the spirit is that gives it: when such a view is acknowledged and accepted, then will there be less fanaticism, and persons will receive communications from spirits for their own intrinsic worth.

Some spirits return and state that in the spirit world flowers grow, and that at times they can bring them to friends, but such flowers vanish quickly, as they are only spiritual, and cannot be seen by any person but those who have their spiritual gifts unfolded. We cannot see it possible for material things to be taken to the spirit world, neither can we see it possible for the productions of spirit life to be tangible for any great length of time in the material life; spirits can without doubt materialize for the time being anything they desire, but it is not the production of spirit life and it will be only of temporary duration in the form of materialization.

At the present time there are so many difficult things to solve in regard to the spirit manifestations and the laws governing them, also there are so many things practised under the guise of spiritualism which is simply deception, that it is difficult to distinguish the true from the false, or whether the manifestations originate from the mundane or the supermundane spheres. "Try the spirits."

The investigator has much to do with the reliability of their communications : a person with a strong determined will can destroy the harmony of any seance, or the reliability of any communication to themselves and others : investigators in visiting mediums should learn that all the manifestations must be given through a natural law, and that harmony is essential in producing spirit manifestations of different forms. Positiveness is beneficial when in the right, but in seeking truth it often proves detrimental to conditions, passivity being far preferable. Persons can remain passive and still not believe until fully convinced. There is too much belief in the world with too little knowledge for that belief.

Individuals going into the presence of sensitives will be most likely to transfer their own troubles and conditions upon the sensitive ; if they have deception in their minds they will be almost sure to get that in return ; if truth, they will attract truth : many mediums act as mirrors or are sponge-like, absorbing or reflecting others' conditions just as they are, and not what they seem to be on the surface ; therefore if such mediums are not well sustained, or if they do not have good surroundings and conditions, the investigator only gets his own thoughts, and nothing reliable from the spirit world is obtained. For illustration a powerful psychologist can project his own imaginations or thoughts upon his sensitive subjects in a manner that they will see and act as he desires or wills them to do, they having no power within themselves to resist his influence. This being a fact it is wisdom to know that the individual possessing the power over us to be in all ways honorable and possessing high moral integrity and principle, before allowing them to gain the control.

Psychological power exercised from the mundane spheres has much to do with the control of some mediums, therefore caution is needed in this direction, as this power is injurious if not put to some beneficial use.

Most spiritualists accept all the seeming inconsistencies and imperfections connected with the spiritual philosophy as they do all under growth that exists in mundane spheres of life; not approving of all the undeveloped conditions in either sphere of existence; but deal with facts and truths as they find them, not expecting to change the laws governing the universe by belief. Having full conviction of the truthfulness of spiritualism we make known some of the imperfections connected with it and give our explanations, not for the purpose of retarding the cause, but to give facts that we have discovered from close observation, knowing that the cause cannot be overthrown by truth itself, but will be enhanced and better understood thereby.

Alchemy, magic or superstition—which? We have been led by spirit power, intuitively or otherwise to discover many strange coincidents without special pains. A peculiar incident occurred more than ten years ago in New York city: an elderly lady engaged in philanthropic work in the city made our acquaintance; she revealed to us a secret that she "dared not reveal to her own children," that she was in possession of a rare, ancient book which claimed to give the key to the "philosopher's stone." She was impressed to show it to us, and also desired us to dispose of it for her without informing either of her children. We called on her at several different times; her family moving in good society to all appearance. We took the book to our rooms and read and re-read it, but could not make any practical sense out of it: the price of the book was one hundred dollars. We kept it for several months, and being considered so valuable by the lady, returned it. Since that time the lady has joined her husband in spirit life; she informed us that she was knowing to her husband's manufacturing "gold" which she sold to bankers in New York, they buying it for the genuine article, and never discovered to the contrary, and she believed it pure. Her husband in the last years of his life was considered insane, often going without food or sleep for weeks. It was at one of these tines that he made the gold, which she said was done by the use of different kinds of ingredients, placing them in a dark room, marking a circle with chalk on the floor, in which figures were written, the ingredients inside. Cabalistic words were spoken, prayers uttered and pure gold would appear in bars ready for the market. The whole modus operandi was given in the book, but we could not work up faith enough to experiment or buy the book. That the lady was sincere in her claims we did not question. We showed the book to several scientific individuals, but they declined to advance money on it, their faith being too weak in her claims.

Another mysterious case was related to us years ago in Bridgeport, Conn. Dr. Styles, a clairvoyant, informed us that he was quite poor and owed small bills, when a voice spoke to him and said "Go and pay your bills." He refused to go without money, but after many promises from the voice he obeyed, and while on the way some ninety dollars in gold was placed in his pocket with a chink while walking. A druggist doing business there corroborated the statement, and said that he received some of it in settlement. This gold coin was claimed to have been brought in the same way that the material flowers are brought, and must have been taken unlawfully from the owner.

Of late we listened to a lecture on "Occultism, Magic and Elementary Spirits" which was so much mixed up with genuine spiritualism that it was difficult to understand what the late converted champion to the subject was attempting to prove ; but in his remarks it was impossible for us to distinguish the different phenomena that he describes as being different from that which is said to be seen while under the effects of strong drink, "delirium tremens", or while under the psychological influence. In the latter the operator can make his subject see or do anything he wills him to do ; while in fact it is only in the imagination of the subject that the articles and beings are seen, while in the former the effects that liquor produces upon the brain causes the individual to see all forms of hideous monsters, undeveloped spirits, or "elementary spirits". Doubtless there are persons that possess the subtle power when in the presence of sensitives, that causes invisibles to impress or make them see whatever they choose, but we understand that the public cannot see the imaginary things ; none but those under the influence of the person possessing the power see the sights. The lecturer said it was capable of being learned, it is the same with psychology by some persons, but if elementary spirits exist they must be seen the same as human spirits, or else it is simply hallucination or imagination in the subject alone, as we see it.

A bad feature in this subject is the secresy subjoined on the whole thing. We saw nothing described in the lecture but what spirits of different grades of development are capable of performing, that is if they are capable of materializing themselves in different sizes and costumes. We have not a doubt but what there is a natural magical power existing in the universe, but that a class of diakka or elementary spirits exist that can perform great wonders, are better informed and can control life elements to higher perfection than can human spirits, we do not believe. We think that such a theory is not only erroneous, but greatly disturbs and retards the spiritualistic philosophy from being accepted by thinking minds. Suppose that spiritualists should attempt to explain all the visions of snakes, beasts and "creeping things" that were said to have been seen by seers in ancient times, and claim them to have been simply elementaries playing their pranks upon poor weak humanity in that age. If the elementary spirits can do what human spirits cannot, why give them this undeveloped name? Why not call them Gods and end the controversy? No question but what the spirit world's inhabitants are exceedingly in earnest, and if they cannot be recognized in a sensible way, they will make the very "stones cry out," and intelligent persons will see things in different ways and forms, and will change their views as sights are presented to them from the spirit world; and they will vacillate from one view to another until the public will lose confidence in them, while they may be honest in what they advocate or see. This may be one of the ways designed by the spirits to attract attention to the subject and their identity, and when once recognized by the world at large, their diabolical work will have served their purpose.

We have no doubt that much of the success or misfortune that exists to-day is largely the effects produced from the spirit world.

While this lecture was being delivered, a Baptist minister in Boston who was educated for the stage, argued that miracles were not suspended. "The form is only changed. You are God's instruments, and you can work miracles."

If both of these men agree and are not mistaken, and sunshine and storms and also trees and fruit can be produced at the word of mortal command, thus overreaching natural law as understood; does it seem possible or probable that God would see his creatures suffer for material want, especially if they are ignorant but worthy? The severe storms and hurricanes that sweep from one end of the country to the other, also the thunder and lightning are as much a "miracle" to many persons as spirit manifestations are to others. No doubt but what all these are produced by natural law and capable of explanation in a limited extent by the finite mind.

MIND READING, PSYCHOMETRY AND CLAIRVOYANCE.

Mind reading of late has received the attention of the learned savans; exhibitions have been given in different sections of the country through the instrumentality of different individuals; articles have been secreted by some one in the audience and found by them while they were closely blindfolded. Tests of this kind have been common amongst the spiritualists for the past twenty five years, with the mesmerists and clairvoyants a much longer space of time.

It is astonishing that the popular mind has but just been awakened to the fact that such a gift exists in human life: many persons consider the gift miraculous, but we cannot see it to be but stepping stones to a more extended knowledge in regard to mind, spirit and matter, and governed by natural laws. The miraculous should be lost sight of, and this natural gift utilized for the benefit of mankind. The imperfections existing in the reliability of the gift to-day are not in the law itself, but in the individuals possessing and receiving the gift.

Psychometry is another gift akin or the same as mind reading and clairvoyance. Persons possessing the gift can read individuals' life, thoughts, actions, and can detect by a letter, lock of hair, hand writing or often by an article of clothing the character, peculiarities and chemical forces of the individual. Some persons are so well unfolded in this direction that the name spoken is sufficient to get in rapport with them. We have seen the power or gift tested in many cases, and have no hesitation in pronouncing it a fixed fact beyond controversy. The gift like every thing else, is beneficial when put to its legitimate use. Doubtless the gift is resorted to in cases that have proven unreliable and detrimental, but the gift should not be condemned by those who acknowledge its existence, but should be investigated and made more practical and perfected. Fire, water, magnetism and electricity are agents in man's possession, and if utilized will bless humanity, but if put to uses contrary to reason they will become injurious in their effects. If the gift of psychometry was more known and recognized it would become a valuable agent in selecting men to fill responsible positions; it also would be resorted to by individuals contemplating marriage, showing the chemical adaptation of forces as well as fitness of temperament. The injury originates, if any, in the abuse of the gift; we cannot separate it from spiritual laws, the difference being only in the form of the manifestations.

Spirits dwelling in the material form are seen by clairvoyants at a distance, and it is often claimed by mediums that they are controlled by them to give communications, also that they go to a distance and heal the sick. We do not pretend to give the law governing this phase of spirit control, but cannot doubt the frequency of the fact, that is if human testimony can be relied upon. We are satisfied that spirits embodied in materiality can travel, but to what extent cannot state with any degree of certainty.

We are informed from a reliable source that a spirit purported to control a medium for several years, giving reliable and valuable advice: afterwards it was ascertained that the spirit was living in his material form. No doubt a spirit, knowing the confidence that these ladies had in the individual, was induced to assist them in the way described, under the cover of their friend's name.

Spirits in some cases show wisdom in not leading or deciding positive, but will suggest or assist. A case came under our knowledge where a person pleaded with their spirit friends to advise concerning a business transaction, but without avail. The person afterwards exercised her reason and acted therefrom, the spirit friends rejoicing to think that individuality had not been given up. Without doubt the highest mission of spirits is to suggest, comfort and assist, and not to dictate and command in relation to the work that belongs to the mundane spheres of life. Spirits often warn us of danger and of enemies, save us from suffering, but we should not lose our individuality and self-sustaining power by constantly seeking spirit advice.

Well informed spiritualists know that spirits can and do deceive at times through honest meaning mediums, either to psychologize the mediums and make them do the act, or else do it by a law not yet fully understood. Absolute test conditions have been placed upon some of the mediums who have always been considered honest and reliable, and absolute proofs have been discovered that deceiving was done by some one. This being acknowledged by spiritualists themselves gives the skeptic a chance to ask "What is the good of spiritualism, or what reliance can be placed upon it?" The question might with equal propriety be asked "What is the use of life, or of some injurious things that exist in the material life"? Sensitives who are passive or psychological subjects are not fit persons to get at facts in either sphere of life. The great difficulty to find where the fault lies is evident to all who have investigated life's forces. We know that spirits follow the investigator from one medium to another, and can lead astray as well as aright; also the spirit friends of the skeptic or rogue can prevent the medium from giving a word of truth in relation to their movements, or of their discovering the facts in relation to their actions: often rogues get the most flattering encomiums as to character and good deeds. If these are facts is it strange that some persons in their ignorance shrink from the doctrine, and is there not a great necessity for the public to know how much the spirit philosophy claims?

There are but few individuals living in mundane spheres that realize to any great extent the spirit life in all its varied unfoldments, neither will they until they reach that life, and experience teaches them. Some persons think that there is to be a universal language on earth, but we cannot see that such a language is to be realized until mankind reach spirit life. Spiritualists have great consolation in advocating their philosophy, as their opponents belong to the "don't know" stripe. Asking them a few questions puts them to flight, or they cover themselves with "I don't know." For instance, ask them what positive proof they have that they exist beyond the change "death," or where the spirit goes at death; invariably they answer through faith they believe, not that they have a knowledge; their answer being vague and uncertain. Generally your room is more desirable than your presence, when you question upon such vital subjects, which should affect all humanity.

Spiritualists are often asked the following question: "Why do not the ancient spirits that lived centuries ago visit earth more frequently?" We will answer from our stand-point. We look upon spirit life as being eternally progressive, and when spirits outgrow material conditions or spheres, they pass on to more exalted conditions or spheres, seldom returning except it be in transmitting thoughts or influences to those who have not grown or arrived at their present growth. Individuals standing high in office in material life seldom do much work physically, but those standing in positions under them are the active workers. It seems a rational solution that spirits go on in their progression, being born to higher conditions daily as desire and fitness warrant, just as do individuals who have grown to understanding and power in mundane spheres of life, their influence being felt through their agents.

If all spirit communications proved true and reliable, they and the mediums would be worshipped as idols; it would destroy the general interpretation and acknowledged philosophy of all well informed spiritualists; also it would take away the use of reason and judgment: in fact it could not be accepted by thinking minds; the information must be as reliable or unreliable as the spirits are that give the information, and no more so.

Spiritualism being a verity, it is time that advanced spiritualists should assume the position of *positive knowledge* as far as the fact itself, and not to be constantly seeking tests and signs, but to accept them when they do come, the same as we accept anything else where reason is exercised.

Continually seeking tests and advice from spirits makes individuals vacillating and undecided in action; the truthfulness of spiritualism being settled, it now requires individuals to act with the knowledge obtained in a practical manner: tests and the different manifestations are more to convince skeptics and honest investigators than for the full acknowledged believers. Millions of individuals in this country as well as other countries, some of them the most gifted in all branches of professions, have made public acknowledgment that the manifestations are from an invisible, intelligent source, that there is no accounting for in reason outside of the philosophy of spiritualism.

The most progressive ministers in all denominations are in the ranks of believers; the Trinitarian Congregationalists, as well as other denominations are at the present time preaching the philosophy as being their own, while doctrines as formerly taught, the two would be as different as light is from darkness.

The most influential scientists have recently become shining lights in the way of defending spiritualism as being a scientific fact in nature. Mediums and their works have been like magnets to attract great minds to the subject, and to-day its teachings are looked upon in an entirely different light from what they were when but few dared face the public with what seemed such an absurd doctrine. It also comes in a time when it is very much needed, and solves many heretofore seeming mysteries and problems in human life. It demonstrates to a certainty what no other form of religious belief does, which is a knowledge, not simply a belief and faith in a future life for all mankind, also an individuality after the material change "death"; it proves that the spirit world and its laws are natural and essential, instead of something to be obtained by belief or lost by unbelief. It disabuses individuals of the sectarian idea of an imaginary Heaven and Hell, located they know not where, but still pretend to know the workings of both places, also what will be the future results in case persons do not accept their limited sectarian views of the two localities, and the requisite conditions and belief to obtain them.

Spiritualism shows death to be as natural as birth and the same thing, the former to be birth into spirit life; the one just as essential to complete the full programme of life as the other, therefore when properly understood "robs death of its sting." Death which was considered dark and dismal, but is known to be universal to all, is but the gate of change, which leads to higher unfoldment of human existence. It also reveals the fact that every deed or act, good or bad, is a part of the individual's life's history, and cannot be repented of only in growth or unfoldment to higher conditions of life. Every individual must stand or fall on their own individual self development, or in other words at spirit birth they will be unmasked and all that is false or good will be seen by themselves as do spiritually developed mediums see them while standing in their presence. Some mediums can penetrate beyond the psychological power of persons living in the mundane sphere of life and can read life's actions, habits, and motives as they would an open book. Spiritualism shows that all forms of worship and belief that do not conform to natural law and truth are transient and temporary, and must pass away and give place to those that unite the past with the present, and of necessity continue the link of union with the future. Spiritual gifts are for all ages and all people without respect to nationality, sex or color; equality in the future being the order with all persons, where capacity and conditions are equal. Persons capable of understanding life in this manner will see harmony and law running through all life and things, and will try to be practical in their own conditions and become acting, living monuments to the uplifting of all humanity.

This doctrine recognises but one authority, but appreciates greatness, but not in a tyrannical manner; it being founded on the laws of the universe, all must admit it sooner or later; it also shows that all that exists does so from its causes, which changes as the causes are removed or outgrown; that "heaven" or "hell" are within each individual and not in a fixed locality; harmony and contentment in our own conditions and surroundings makes "heaven," the reverse of it makes "hell"; both spheres of life are subject to these rules and changes. Spiritualism being a fixed fact and the foundation of life, it cannot change its base even if those believing in it differ in understanding it; the abuse of spiritual gifts is more from ignorance and want of spiritual growth in the persons exercising them, than from any other cause. Knowledge will harmonize all differences, the fault not being in the philosophy itself, but in mankind not living up to the highest development that their being is capable of being unfolded into; persons should not be alarmed by undeveloped spirits in either sphere of life, neither should they attempt to war with them; the uplifting of the lower to the higher must be evident to all thinking minds, to be the true mission of life, therefore that of spiritualism.

No doubt but what unprincipled skeptics have attempted to destroy the influence when sitting with a medium or have done something to bring the medium into bad repute; for instance at a public gathering they could unbeknown to any one but themselves drop articles that would be picked up by others, and then the cry would be fraud; the mediums would have no way of proving their innocence until test conditions were applied to them.

We desire to be just, therefore give this information that mediums may not be considered exposed without positive proofs are discovered.

Selfishness is a lower condition of life than unselfishness, and when it does not take on the form of meanness, it is somewhat essential to material spheres of existence, in supporting and caring for self, family and the unfortunates that are in the community; hoarding of money for miserly purposes is but an earth mistake, which the spirit life corrects.

We look upon spirit life as typical of material life, divested of deception and hypocrisy; the material body is exchanged for the spiritual or is thrown aside, the spiritual one appearing of its own necessity, it being the natural order of the change of forms of life on towards completeness, with likes, dislikes, attractions and repulsions the same, the only difference being what the material body attracts or repulses of itself, the spirit being the same in both spheres, enjoying in degree, depending entirely upon the way it lives, and the capacity to overcome and resist temptations that are injurious to itself.

SPIRIT HEALING THE HIGHEST MODE OF TREATMENT. It may be interesting to some persons to know why we compiled and wrote the following named books, which we will describe. In the year 1870 our attention was called by Dr. J. R. Newton, the renowned healer, to the book entitled "Mental Cure," by the inspired writer Rev. W. F. Evans. The Dr. spoke of this work as excelling anything that he had ever read, which illustrated the power of the mind over disease. We obtained a copy and found its philosophy to be in many ways our own experiences, therefore applicable in our own practice to a certain extent; the philosophy of life was clearly and intelligently explained in theory; the practical workings did not seem as definite for magnetists as they were for psychologists.

We were at that time treating disease by the Vital Magnetic Cure process. The Mental Cure book being beyond the understanding of the general reader, spiritual experience and much interior growth must be obtained, either by sickness, trials or experience before the book could be appreciated; but it being high in tone and aim we felt moved upon to extend its sphere of usefulness. We recommended it to persons that we thought would appreciate it, having introduced many copies before becoming personally acquainted with the author; in the meantime compiled a treatise or text-book, giving conditions, rules and laws for applying the natural forces, such as spirit, magnetic and electric to the removal of disease. Our object was to put into practical use what the Mental Cure book had defined in theory.

May 5 1871 we addressed the following questions to the spirit that first convinced us of the truth of spiritualism, "Will the treatise I am about to publish be a success and do much good to humanity?" The letter being closely sealed, the medium's hand in my presence was mechanically controlled and wrote the following answer, which was written back-handed and from right to left, "I am glad to see that you reverence the beautiful philosophy of the spirit unfoldment—glad to see that you endeavor to impress those around you with liberal ideas. You are by so doing receiving a great amount of spirit magnetism—magnetism that soon will unfold to you other gifts.

"You will in the treatise you intend to publish meet with success. Yes, it will do much good; it will benefit mankind generally. I see around you many bright and pure spirits, spirits that can and will, through your organism, make many afflicted souls happy, give relief to the many ills that flesh is heir to. Continue on with the holy work."

We dedicated the treatise to the progressive physicians of the nineteenth century, as it deals with principles and laws that belong to all individuals, as far as they understand and can utilize them. The rules given in the Vital Magnetic Cure book are as full and explicit as they can be made practical to different individuals. In compiling the work we investigated and read all available books that treated upon the subject; also obtained from spirit intelligences knowledge that has been demonstrated as practical, in our own and many others' experiences and practice. We found that animal magnetism, psychology, mesmerism, clairvoyance and psychic force was clearly defined, but there seemed to be a step beyond, which needed more general information.

Much that goes for spirit magnetic treatment is psychological influence. The public should know that there is a difference between them. Some persons have much healing force, who have but little or no psychological power of their own; others have psychological power but lack the healing element, and often unconsciously impart it to the patient, which has to be broken away from, if detrimental, before a cure can be effected; and many times the sickness is simply the results of a psychological power that is not beneficial. We have never thought it wisdom to attempt to hold psychological control of the minds of patients, except when unbalanced; we have in such cases found more lasting benefit by changing the system chemically, than by the use of the will power alone. In unfoldment of spiritual gifts it seems wrong to me to use a will power upon the subject. Many persons have no spiritual gifts that can be unfolded, even if they desire them ever so much; and it seems a waste of time to try, as it does in attempting to learn children to sing, play, draw, and to develop other attainments in those who have no natural talent in that direction.

We have been more particularly drawn to the subject of spirit or vital magnetism, therefore have endeavored to harmonize what has previously been discovered, with what is so well demonstrated in the present time under the name of spirit forces. There is not a magnetizer, healer or clairvoyant of any degree of experience, but what acknowledges the law, conditions and suggestions made in this treatise to be correct from facts and principles.

In the work we connected the link of the chain that binds the past with the present, giving the experiences (from history) of different persons who have exercised their gifts, commencing as far back as Elijah and Elisha, and on to Mesmer's time, giving the French Commissioners' report, Benjamin Franklin being one of the number. Persons in every age express their own views, conclusions and experiences.

We take no credit of having discovered new laws or

any new power, but the general conclusions and suggestions in the treatise may be new to many.

When modern spiritualism became known it brought with it a solution of animal magnetism, psychology, mesmerism, spirit magnetism and magic which harmonizes the past with the present, and shows that it must continue on to more perfection, thus proving the words of Jesus to be true, where it states in the fourteenth chapter of John that spirit magnetic healing had not advanced to its highest state of perfection. It is not supernatural but natural, and can be cultivated when latent in the individual.

Many of the old school practitioners are acknowledging the beneficial results from the use of vital magnetism; others who are bigoted are endeavoring in all ways to stop its use; making laws that make it a criminal offence, or imposing a fine upon those who dare to use it. We cannot see any cause for alarm on the part of true principled magnetists, but with the old school practitioners do see a shaking among the "dry bones."

Doubtless spirit healing will be one of the most useful phases of the spiritual philosophy, and be the means of drawing the public to the practical benefits of the subject. Once convinced that spiritualism is a verity, the next work is to utilize it for the benefit of mankind.

It has been suggested that magnetists and clairvoyants should organize as do other medical practitioners, grant diplomas etc. We see no gain to be derived from such a movement, as there are no body of individuals capable of taking such a responsibility; diplomas must come from nature, which is in adapted individual organisms; mankind cannot limit or grant the power, neither can it be bought or sold. It is beyond the power of institutions made by men. Persons possessing the gifts cannot be prevented, for any length of time, from using them in this country when occasion and duty requires.

A law to prevent unprincipled persons from obtaining money by false pretences and deception now exists in most of the States, and can be applied in all professions and trades, which is proper and commendable.

The design of this treatise being to make the public better acquainted with what can and is being done by the use of the subtle forces, and to show the laws and conditions requisite for their practical use, also to show that there is nothing in exercising the forces to be ashamed of, or in individuals employing healers when sick in this age, more than there was in the past.

The work is adapted alike to both operator and patient: the sick and well need to know life's laws and their effects. Much suffering is prevented by knowing the laws: many persons doctor themselves sick, never attempting to know the laws of health.

After a practice of more than four years since it was written, we see no reason to change the statements therein made, they being satisfactorily demonstrated daily. Within a short time several purported "renowned" spirits have given their views in relation to vital magnetism, which fully corroborate with the facts published in the book four years previous; thus showing that this work is reliable, and that we were in harmony with them, or that the spirits err in judgment and have been biased by the mundane sphere.

There exists without a doubt, a vitalizing spirit force in nature, that can be utilized for the benefit of the sick and afflicted ; individuals possessing the gift to do good should have the benefit to the patient more prominent than the hoarding of money from the use of their gifts.

The treatise takes the positive spiritual stand-point; other works had failed to give a *spiritual* interpretation either from policy or otherwise. Some of the individuals are using spiritual gifts and deny their master, or will not acknowledge that they are assisted by spirits or spirit forces, and when questioned upon the subject refuse to use the word spirit, while they at the same time are controlled or go to those who are under spirit guidance, and ask of them counsel.

If spirit is superior and more potent than materiality, why should we be ashamed to acknowledge its existence or its use? Spirit magnetism does not perform miracles, neither does it make the old young, except to feel so in spirit; or prevent the change "death" coming to all persons alike, in the onward march of time.

The human system is continually changing; magnetism that will assist to-day may not to-morrow, but may in the future. In ancient times healers were persecuted and questioned for healing on the sabbath day, but in this generation there is no particular day which is universally considered sacred by all nations and people. Every day in the week is considered a sabbath day or day of rest by some nation or sect of people, and is as sacred to them as other days are to other religious organizations; therefore we have come to the conclusion that all days are equally sacred, but that it is wisdom and advisable to devote one particular day in seven for a day of rest and instruction, and it would be better to have all people fix upon the same day, that one sect may not disturb the others. The Bible record does not show that healers and religious teachers had titles attached to their names, neither were they educated under any particular form of religious belief, or at any renowned institution of learning. They did not use chemicals, stimulants or artificial means to unfold their spiritual gifts; the power came upon them unsought and when least expected. Adaptation and preparation as to conditions, and in coming in rapport with individuals who possessed spiritual gifts quickened the latent forces in persons who possessed it naturally, but in a dormant state. It must be evident that the same law works in this age in degree. The only trouble with mankind has been to look to the past for the whole truth, instead of the present for its share.

There are many reasons to-day why spirit magnetism is unpopular, and prejudice exists with the unthinking mind. First there are persons favored with the "gift of healing," who are using it successfully under other names (sugar coated,) therefore no credit is given to its true origin; others are palming off the use of sponge baths, inhalation, chemical batteries etc., all no doubt good in their place and time, and often work in harmony, but should be credited to their own mode of treatment, rather than be styled magnetic healing; second, many finding it an easy way of getting into business without capital, put up their sign and style themselves "Dr." and commencing practice without experience, and perhaps half developed and with very little power, but much assurance, and in some cases performing cures. This gives them encouragement, and they go on and at times live a life which is objectionable to good society, thus bringing disgrace upon the noble cause they are engaged in. The unthinking public look upon these undeveloped actions and forget the cures made, and condemn the entire system of practice. Many, no doubt, are engaged without power trying to get a living in healing the sick, who doubtless could serve humanity better if they were engaged in a calling more fitted to their growth and adaptation. Also there are many who possess the gift of healing who will not use it on account of its being unpopular, and in the hands of the uneducated and unprincipled in some cases.

It should be distinctly understood that no two healers' forces are alike, and no two can work alike. What one can do another may or may not, and that each person engaged in the work should stand or fall upon his or her individual merits, and be judged from their acts and works individually, just the same as it is with the "regular" practice of medicine. Some are gifted, others less so. In this acknowledgment it only shows that the law and mode of practice is not at fault, but the blame, if any, is in the persons engaged in a work that they are not fitted to fill. The power should be acknowledged by all who possess it, also be cultivated by a class of individuals who are honest and willing to work for humanity "for the good they can do" more than to have money the first and last motive.

The object of these last remarks is to show a class of persons who possess the power and are ashamed to use it, that the law and system of practice itself is all right, but the fault is with the individuals engaged in the work, also to encourage good persons to "covet the best gifts" and make the system of practice what it should be, respectable and above all, useful; then will medical men, and also those who make our laws not only be obliged to acknowledge it, but protect those engaged in the practice, and place it upon an equal footing with other modes of medical treatment, that dare not compete with it.

The same remarks will apply with equal force to other spiritual gifts and their use. It should be understood that philosophy and speculative theories about the use of spiritual gifts are all very well, but without the power but little beneficial results will follow.

MAGNETIZED PAPER and other materials as a vehicle for transmitting spirit or vital magnetic force to patients at a distance is without question a fixed fact in the laws of life which has in the past and present been demonstrated fully to the minds of many persons. It is strange how individuals can believe that Paul magnetized handkerchiefs etc. in his day, and healed the sick at a distance, and doubt living witnesses who know the power still exists to-day.

Doubtless disease and inharmony can be transmitted in the same manner that the healing element is imparted, each person sending their own peculiar forces, differing in quality, as the persons differ in their elements, attractions and mode of living, who impart the forces.

Without question persons who are spiritually unfolded in their being, and have adapted organisms, are the most successful in making cures by this mode of treatment. Persons may send "magnetic paper" who have little or no power for healing the sick, and if the public are not better informed concerning the difference, the world will be filled with "magnetized paper" and thereby bring reproach upon this system of practice.

A sensitive lady remarked to me thus: "I should be afraid to use magnetized paper prepared by those I know nothing of their mode of life or influence." The remarks spoke volumes to us, and gives our views in relation to this form of treatment, which is precisely the same as it is with personal treatment by different magnetizers. We could cite most wonderful cures produced by vitalized paper and letters, but refrain as the public is not ready to accept them.

We have known infant children to be cured at a distance by the use of vital magnetized paper. This takes it beyond the realms of mind, faith or imagination, and establishes it as a potential healing force that is conveyed by the paper. Faith may assist in producing better conditions with some persons, but after all the subtle power exists, independent of faith.

The spirit healing element differs from animal magnetism, psychological force and the rubbing process, various religious sects calling it by different names, such as "prayer cure", using ointment and words in the name of Jesus; others use "holy water" and prepared "wafers." Doubtless all of these are means used to harmonize and give faith to the patient, producing conditions that the intelligent invisibles may come in better rapport with the patient that they may use the healing element in nature, which differs in each operator and patient as they are prepared to receive, and all of the different modes of spirit healing originate from spirits and the spirit world, whether publicly admitted or not.

Persons who take an interest in the philosophy of health and the cure of disease should investigate the subject personally.

We had no sooner finished Vital Magnetic Cure book than there seemed to be another work for us, and could not feel at rest until we had written and compiled another book which we entitled "Nature's Laws in Human Life, an Exposition of Spiritualism." Perhaps "Spiritualism on Trial" would have been a more appropriate title, and have expressed its mission better. We took the position that spiritualism being natural and a verity, it was capable of being demonstrated, and no fear from the clearest and closest investigation and criticism; desiring to be fair and honest in seeking after truth, and in this way knew of no better way than to collate distinguished individuals' opinions, *pro* and *con*, who had expressed their views upon the subject, and place these opinions in one book, that the reader might get at the different views entertained, and in this way come to a clearer understanding than it was possible to obtain by reading but one side of the subject. We knew that spiritualism must stand or fall upon its own merits, therefore without fear or favor wrote and compiled the work named.

This treatise takes up the law of mediumship, the conditions requisite for unfoldment or development, as far as the most advanced minds have proven to be practical; also the reliability of communications, seances or circles, their formation, and the rules and laws to obtain manifestations; also quotations from the Bible, which proves spiritualism to be the key that explains the seeming mysteries contained therein.

Conclusions are drawn upon the social question that has foisted itself upon spiritualism proper. We have left the subject an open question, that the readers might sit in judgment as jurors, taking the testimony brought to bear on the question as evidence pro and con.

Individuals must settle this question for themselves; it is worse than folly to attempt to make converts against their convictions; persons must feel it to be a truth before they can in sincerity say "I do believe." Evidence given by others is not as convincing as when it comes personally to self.

When we hear persons repeat over the tests that have been given to others, it does not have the weight of evidence that it does when a person says I have seen such and such things for myself, and I know what I am talking or writing about from personal knowledge. Other persons' testimony may do to corroborate what we have witnessed. Persons who have been fully satisfied of its truthfulness should make charitable allowance for the honest skeptic. Most spiritualists in their first investigation were skeptical; one well convinced spiritualist is worth a thousand of the vacillating, "milk and water" ones, who at times do not know whether they believe or not. Undecided opinions with its advocates does but little to convince the public that there is a reality beyond controversy. We sincerely believe that individuals who oppose spiritualism are warring against themselves, and in time will acknowledge that they were working against the author of their being and the law of life.

This work has convinced persons who have never witnessed a manifestation or had a personal test, the evidence being more convincing in its favor than could be brought against it. The book is well adapted for a missionary work.

SOCIAL FREEDOM AN OBSTACLE TO SPIRITUALISM. In the spring of 1874 our mind was particularly called to the "social freedom" doctrine, which seemed to take the principal interest of spiritualists' meetings, and brought reproach and disgrace upon the true philosophy of the subject, as we understood it; therefore we collated and published a twenty five cent pamphlet, containing all available evidence that favored law and order, as well as a high state of morals and civilization in the social relations, and compared them with the freedomite teachings.

The title of the pamphlet is "An Exposition of Social Freedom: Monogamic Marriage the highest development of Sexual Equality." The following criticism, from a prominent attorney-at-law, will give the reader some idea of the important character of this work:

"I read the pamphlet with much interest, and I not only greatly admire the views, tone and sentiment, but I may truly say that there are indeed but very few ideas in the whole book that I do not concur in. I think the views enunciated in the pamphlet are practical, sensible, and wise; the sentiment is healthy, the tone is catholic and charitable, and such as to commend it to all thinking minds."

The time is fast approaching when equality before the law will be recognized alike by male and female as far as practical: there never will come a time, as we see it, that all individuals will be equal in capacity and power. Every individual must fill their own position and work out their own destiny; that which makes woman guilty makes man equally so. A man prostitute is no better than a woman prostitute; it is only the opinions of the public that makes him appear so. When young girls are forced to submit to prostitution or be deprived of work, it is time that such employers are exposed and branded by public opinion as unworthy of respect or confidence; thousands there be on the sensual plane of development, and who are paving the way to the downfall of innocent victims.

The fascinating doctrine of "social freedom" has some truth and much error, therefore it has without doubt caused much inharmony in the spiritualists' ranks, wrecking (for the time being) many well meaning persons, but as one extreme follows another, without question their better judgment will predominate and eradicate all false views concerning human life and its use and destiny.

One of the radical Unitarian ministers of Boston in a late lecture made use of the following language in relation to the creed of one of the self-claimed leaders of the "social freedom" doctrine, "It leads to irreligion, misanthropy, murder and ruin." If such opinions are entertained against the teachings by those claiming to be radical, what can the conservative element think of them? Words are cheap; actions are what determine individuals' integrity and character. "The tree is known by his fruit."

Doubtless much of the cause that produces inharmony in society at the present time is intermarriage with different nationalities, the chemical elements and influences being antagonistic. Time may harmonize all society, but while it is passing through the developing and spiritualizing process, inharmony must be the effect as a natural consequence. Such conditions should not be advocated as being superior to a higher growth.

The public have looked upon spiritualism as being the father and mother of the "social freedom" doctrine. We felt satisfied that it belonged to society in general, without regard to religious belief, and that the world should not mistake it for the teachings of spiritualism proper.

Since publishing this work the editor of a paper devoted to the advocacy of promiscuity or unrestrained passions, and the doing away with all man made laws to govern marriage, making society free and common, has defined "social freedom" in a way that no one of sense need err in its understanding. He accuses a lecturer of not only preaching their doctrine, but practising it, stating what the acts are that constitute their philosophy, which is admitted by the individual, while at the same time he says he has seen his folly and abandoned the mode of life. The paper contains comments upon the recantation, and rejoices to think that there may be in the future a prospect of his returning to his former mode of life, which he no doubt fell into while under a psychological delusion. What are such teachings but the advocacy of prostitution and promiscuity under another name?

ANIMALS SUSCEPTIBLE TO SPIRIT INFLUENCE AND DISEASES. Animals doubtless are affected by spirits and spirit influence; our experience so far goes to show that dogs more than other animals are susceptible to spirit influence. It is said that the beast and hogs were controlled by spirits, in the past. Does not the same law hold good in the present?

We could give many instances that have come under our personal observation that would warrant us in making the assertion, that it is a fact that cannot be overthrown; a few of them will suffice to establish it.

Some more than two years ago a man well known in Boston passed on to spirit life; he resided in a public building, occupied the only tenement at that time; his wife and son about fourteen years of age were the only persons that remained in the building the night after his departure. In the night they heard a noise in the entry leading to their tenement, they being timid did not go to the door; in the morning they found a strange dog lying at the door of the room that contained the body of the husband and father. As soon as the door was opened the dog jumped about and seemed delighted, and showed as much rejoicing as was possible to manifest: he remained with them while they stopped in the building. The dog recognized persons who called upon them; those who had selfish motives he would bark at, and behave entirely the opposite from what he did when persons called that had no pecuniary selfish interest, thus showing conclusively that either the spirit of the husband and father, or some of his or their spirit friends were influencing the dog.

They gave the dog away at several different times, but the dog would not leave them until they left the building, always returning as soon as set at liberty. They never saw the dog before that night, and it has been a mystery how he obtained an entrance to the building. He has never been seen by them since. We saw the dog and noticed its intelligent actions.

Soon after leaving the city, the widow having occasion to visit it, on returning about nine o'clock in the evening she was met at the horse car by a large, noble looking dog. He seemed to recognize her and started off by her side, taking some of her clothing into his mouth. After seeing her safe to the door he passed on through the yard, she not seeing him since nor before that time. The lady called the family to the door to see the dog as he left the yard; he proved to be a strange dog to them. Our information was obtained from the lady, who is reliable; she had no object in falsifying.

Another case, a young man in Syracuse, N. Y. was thrown into the canal by another person while engaged in a quarrel, and was drowned. He had two pet dogs who would at times run and bark, and acted otherwise strangely. The mother and sister of the young man visited Moravia; the son and brother appeared materialized, as life-like as though he had been in the material form. He spoke of the dogs, and how he influenced them to act in the manner described, which the mother acknowledged was truthful; the medium was an entire stranger to the ladies and knew nothing of the dogs or their actions.

We witnessed this and heard the conversation by the materialized young man, also the mother's acknowledgment. There were twenty other witnesses to the circumstances; there could not have been any deception or collusion practised between the parties. Mediums often see and describe dogs; whether it be done by spirit friends, or the spirit of the dog presents itself is a question not fully settled with us.

Still another case: a dog was lying down quietly while a conversation was going on between two persons, the subject being the peculiar actions of a medium while she was in the material form. The medium in question was eccentric in many ways, doing many things that well disciplined persons disapproved of; whether the actions were done by spirits controlling the medium or the acts originated with the medium herself is a question. At any rate they were acts to be discountenanced, let them originate in either sphere of life. We do not say that the medium was to blame; there might have been elements in her organism that attracted impractical unfortunate spirits, but to the facts in the case; as soon as the discussion became animated, the dog commenced to bark and behaved strangely. We ordered the dog to leave the room, at the same time advancing with a *will* towards him. He left for the rear part of the house, and when we had stated to the person that it was either the spirit of the medium or the spirits that influenced her while in the material body, that was causing the dog to become so boisterous, the dog became quieted and came back and laid himself down as he was at first; thus establishing the fact to us of the power of spirits to control dogs.

We had within one year broken the control that this medium had consciously or unconsciously thrown upon three different persons; doubtless the control was broken upon the dog in the same manner.

With this medium it was difficult to distinguish whether the injurious effect was performed by a controlling influence or done by her own spirit; it does not seem wisdom for spiritualists to approve of actions performed by these erratic, fanatical mediums or set them up as leaders worthy of imitation. Individuals having in their own natures and organisms idiosyncrasies, or who attract influences of that nature, should be considered as unfortunates instead of benefactors. This explanation seems consistent with the true spiritual philosophy. Dogs are known to take upon themselves disease. An acquaintance has had two dogs within a short time; one of them died, the other is entirely changed in its forces; formerly quiet, but now nervous and shows signs of disease, and without doubt will share the fate of the other; the owner of them improving in health as the dogs sicken. This shows that disease as well as influences can be imparted to dogs.

INFLUENCES AND DISEASE IMPARTED TO CHILDREN. Children playing together often transmit or partake of influences from one another; for instance, a beautiful quiet child eighteen months of age was playing with one three years of age; the latter was boisterous and excitable; would jump and scream, in fact the parents could not control him. As soon as the two children came together, the quiet one became as restless and boisterous in proportion to its age as the other. It is now more than two years since the children first met; the excited state continues, the parents being much exercised over the child's actions, and are satisfied that the first cause of the excitement was the influence imparted or transmitted from the excited child; the child is uncommonly bright and promising; with this exception she would be considered quite remarkable in her growth of development.

We will quote another case of what might be called obsession, a negative mediumistic lady who had incurable consumption fastened upon her; while under the influence of some unruly spirit she would threaten her attendants, and talk in a rough swearing manner to those who visited her; after the influence had left her she would cry and feel mortified to think that she had been made an instrument of such undeveloped influences. We were called to visit the lady, and with one magnetic treatment the influence was dispossessed, and months afterwards she passed to spirit life as peacefully as one would in going to sleep, with no more trouble from the undeveloped spirit. We could relate many similar cases, but this is sufficient to illustrate the points involved.

Persons visiting low, undeveloped conditions or influences take upon themselves these influences and will carry the influences to sensitives, they feeling and acting as the persons do who first impart them. A human being, an animal or a material substance can be the vehicle to transmit the influence to the sensitive. There are doubtless influences that have not been individualized, that can be transmitted to sensitives, and much sorrow and injury created thereby.

While in a western city a lady called on us with her son some ten years of age. She said that she had visited physicians far and near to see if her son could not be benefited; he had no teeth. We frankly informed her that the boy was not born natural, and that her money might benefit the physicians, but that they could not bring natural teeth into his jaw. She then related the circumstances connected with her while the child was passing through ante-natal life. Her dentist called her into his office to see a young man without teeth; it proved to be her milkman, and every morning on seeing him, the toothless jaw would appear to her in imagination, and when her boy was born he had precisely such a toothless jaw as the young man had. This is proof positive that impressions can be imparted to the mother which does affect her unborn child.

Last summer we met an old man of seventy eight years of age, who was remarkably active and healthy; he gave a history of his birth and life, which was interesting and useful to the world; therefore in this connection we place it before the public, that others may profit by it. He was the youngest of ten children; the parents and the rest of the children found an early grave by the disease consumption. His theory was that while all the rest of the children partook of nourishment from the mother, he was brought up on cow's milk, therefore did not partake of the mother's disease. This case speaks volumes to the fact of partaking of disease by nourishment.

Sorrow, grief and disease can be transmitted to others by and through the law of sympathy. No question but what birds are influenced by human spirits.

If any part of the human organism is diseased, it affects other parts; anything that disturbs mind or body affects the life forces of the entire system, and disease is generated thereby; therefore individuals of a sensitive nature cannot be too careful of their surroundings, especially when amongst conflicting elements. Our object at this time is to show to the public that spiritualists do not claim that the lives of mediums in this age are better or worse than they were in Bible times, that is without their acts show the fact. The law is one and the same thing in all ages, let it be good, bad or indifferent; it is not for us to find fault with the law, but it is for us to see that proper use is made of the laws governing us and others, and not abuse them. Doubtless there are many claiming to be spirit mediums who have not sufficient power or development to meet the demands of skeptics, or even of the full believer; others who do not seem to be of any benefit to themselves or the cause, and it would be far better for them and the cause if they were engaged in business more adapted to their growth and mode of living. Many of these advertise largely; strangers to the cause call upon them and not getting satisfaction they go away, not knowing the difference between the genuine and false or undeveloped mediums; jump to a hasty conclusion, and pronounce the whole subject a humbug or a delusion, not even stopping to consider that there may be the true as well as the false.

Mediums that are unfolded outside of seances or without any thought on their part, either through sickness or without any seeming exertion, are generally the most practical; spirit gifts are often unfolded by spirits who do not use judgment, and often in individuals who do not know the first thing concerning the law of control. The M. Ds. in many cases not recognizing spirit control, often suggest their confinement in an insane asylum. These being facts that are becoming quite frequent, it is time that the public should know all that there is to be known concerning the highly important subject of mediumship and its effects and laws. "Many spirit mediums are called but few are chosen." The reason must be evident to all who are well informed and know the lack of knowledge in the laws governing the entire subject.

Many mediums become impractical in all their movements, therefore do not succeed in using their gifts. It does not seem advisable for individuals to abandon material labor until they are prepared for the spiritual work. Some mediums that are in the field, that of labor, are not so from choice and the good they can do, but because they cannot find any other employment that is as profitable with the same amount of capital invested. If such are the facts the spirits are obliged to do their work, also control the mediums against their will, which makes unfavorable conditions. With all the wild schemes that have been foisted upon spiritualism proper, it still moves on with a steady gradual growth, its foundation stones being facts and truths, it must continue on to more perfection.

The local papers to-day do not condemn the entire subject for the individual acts of its believers, and often spiritualists are to blame, as in the following instance. A skeptical editor in Bangor, Maine, visited the seance of a noted medium. He wrote several questions directed to spirits in the form. No response came; this made it a grand test, convincing him that the medium did not make it. As soon as the medium and his friends discovered that he had been trifling, as they termed it, they became offended, thus destroying all the good effect that had been accomplished in this case. There is no fixed way to "convert" all people, and it is much the better way to let every one come into the "fold" in their own way and good time. Doubtless persons may be true, good and honest, at the same time have erroneous views in regard to the future life, and the means of obtaining it: a great work has been accomplished within a few years in establishing this fact. Spiritualists have been considered inconsistent by some persons, therefore we print the following items for the purpose of showing the public that the tables can be turned.

CHURCH PREJUDICE.—BIBLE IN PUBLIC SCHOOLS. A case of religious bigotry occurred during the last war, which we mention for the purpose of illustrating. In the city of Philadelphia the evangelical churches united in sanitary organization to assist in caring for the sick and wounded soldiers, and without doubt done a noble work; the spiritualists offered their services as citizens and were willing to work with them, but were rejected on account of their religious belief. We happened to be in the city at the time and called on one of the ministers; his wife speaking of the good that the organization was doing, also alluded to spiritualists (not knowing that we were one) offering to join them in their christian work; she thought they should not be allowed to work with them, etc.

Dr. H. T. CHILD, the veteran spiritualist, organized an independent band composed of spiritualists, and proceeded to the field of battle and bloodshed, performing a glorious, noble work. The soldiers have reason to be thankful to this band of spiritualists for the care and attention rendered them during their great need.

Doubtless to-day such bigotry would not be shown in such a case of need, spiritualism having become more popular. Both the minister and his wife are now inhabitants of spirit life where they have doubtless discovered that dogmas, creeds and ceremonies are non-essentials with them in their new home.

The different evangelical churches jointly agree on Jesus' death and his atoning blood as the only way to obtain eternal life and happiness, and without this belief no one is saved, while at the same time there is no harmony between them. Certain dogmas some think essential, others do not: but of late they are endeavoring to work together on common ground, as they no doubt see that if they do not agree here they will not in spirit life. • If spiritualists were as inconsistent as they have been they might well be considered a credulous, deluded people. The following verse in the last chapter of St. Mark has caused much misunderstanding. "He that believeth and is baptized shall be saved, but he that believeth not shall be damned." Believe what? The rest of the chapter states conclusive and shows that it has no reference to eternal punishment or of gaining eternal life. It states that Jesus materialized himself, and those witnessing him did not believe it was him. He then said to them that certain "signs should follow them that believe."

There is not a member belonging to said churches who dare try the test of belief recorded in the same chapter, and said to be laid down by Jesus himself. Do his words mean anything, and is not the entire chapter an account of spirit manifestations, the same that is witnessed in this age?

"Damned" and "saved" have various interpretations, but the modern one in the connection used would be condemned, retarded for the former word, saved from error in the latter, thereby receiving the truth which was demonstrated in deed and act through Jesus. Being baptized without doubt referred to spirit and not water, as the whole chapter has a spiritual significance. Persons healing the sick, drinking deadly things and handling poisonous serpents doubtless have spirit assistance and protection. Baptism by water will not answer in such cases. The sitting on the right or left hand of God must be with witnesses speculative, and shows that Jesus at that time was not considered God, or equal with him, either by his friends or himself. It distinctly says in the Bible that no one has ever seen God; in another place it says that persons walked and talked with him; which are we to believe?

A Christian minister preaching Christ and him crucified as being the only means of gaining eternal life, also teaching sunday school scholars the practical results of an honest upright life, while at the same time forging other persons' names, and soon after fleeing the country, seems to be the last exhibition of a wolf in sheep's clothing; this same minister being a politician using his influence to enact a law that would drive spiritualism from the State. Such acts show how thin the professed religious covering is with many who make long prayers to be heard of men, while in fact it is resorted to as a cover for undeveloped actions, swindling and the like.

If the doctrine of one hundred years ago was correct, and that belief in the sectarian dogmas and creeds saved souls, and those not believing in them were lost or to be burned up in hell, why are they not true to-day, or why such a modification in the teachings by the same denominations? If it has been discovered that a mistake has been made, why sail under the old flag of error or still retain the crude dogmas in their creeds? We would say preach the *old* until it becomes so offensive or ridiculous that reason will assert her convictions, and afterwards be independent, and not be ashamed to sail under the flag of progression, which is spiritualism. Believing in one doctrine and preaching another is hypocrisy, as we see it. A great judgment day is fixed for all persons, and the raising of the material body in the future; a personal devil, a local heaven and hell, is either true or false; if true why go round it; if false why not so proclaim it fearlessly?

Religion to us means daily acts in life; there is no fixed standard for religion, that is allowing belief to constitute the word, but if persons' actions make their religion, doubtless the better they are the higher and purer would be their religion. It will not do to mix the old wine with the new, or attempt to ride two horses at one time, without expecting bad results; it is the same in teaching a new doctrine under an old name, trying to hold on to the old when it is outgrown. It seems inconsistent that a paper that claims to be an advocate of Congregationalism and the saving of souls by the vicarious atonement process, also defaming spirit mediums without investigating their claims, while at the same time advocating the laws and principles that spiritualists have taught for the past twenty five years, which are in direct opposition to the views of the regular Congregationalists' interpretation of life and its laws concerning a future life and its rewards and penalties; also publishing long articles on the rearing of fine high priced colts, seems to us like blending the sublime, the useful and the ridiculous; the mixture combined in such a compound making it appear like a farce to thinking minds. Is it strange that the public are losing confidence in claimed professions, and that some of the religious teachers who have an eye to the "signs of the times" and are somewhat shrewd, see that good persons out of the churches are a great hindrance to the power and example they desire to exert in society, and are suggesting that membership be conferred upon the good, whether they desire it or not; in this way hold or count on *our side* all the good as well as some that prove black sheep. This logic may be well for the church, but it lacks principle, and shows policy more than lasting benefit. We have no doubt but what good persons will take care of themselves let them be members of churches or not. If those not good can be made better by placing them under church bonds, the quicker they are secured the better for society, but indications show that the churches have but little lasting effect upon some persons.

Jesus, according to history, was in full sympathy with the spiritual philosophy, and inferred that there was but one sin but what could be forgiven in this world or the next; this shows that he believed in progression after the change death, or he would not have alluded to forgiveness in the next world. Doubtless he desired to be understood that by resisting or warring against the spirit influx (Holy Ghost) it was something that could not be obtained while doing so, therefore the time lost by so doing could not be regained in spirit life; and when there they would discover that they had sinned against the spirit of truth, and in ages could not arrive to the degree of perfection that they might have done, had they worked in harmony with the laws of life and the universe. When we consider that no two individuals are organized or look alike, is it strange that no two think alike on all subjects?

Abundant evidence is seen to convince any thinking mind that the Great Spirit is no respecter of persons, or any particular form of religious belief; neither does he go outside of universal law to protect, sustain or punish any one. The good and pure suffer by poverty and accident as well as the wicked; churches of all denominations are burned and receive the bad effects of severe storms and high winds alike. Do these facts not show conclusive that the all-wise spirit does not turn aside by the pleadings of mortals. Mankind can change their course of action and belief when they discover the true and better way of living; also must work in harmony with natural laws, instead of having the laws conform to their crude ideas of them; that is if they would be correct in principle and desire harmony.

In a free country where the greatest liberty of religious thought should be tolerated, and where so many different interpretations of the Bible are prominent, it seems child's play or foolishness to attempt to harmonize all shades of opinion upon the Bible; therefore in schools for general teaching in the useful, practical studies necessary for every day life, where the money is obtained for the support of them by an equal taxation of its citizens, it seems not only wisdom, but advisable to either do away with its use or read it as any other history. The various views in relation to its religious interpretation should be taught only in the different organizations, but common school education must be universal or inharmony will exist, as the consequence of diversions. *Our* church should not be taken into consideration in general education.

The ministerial church scandal which has shocked the entire country, and is an elephant to-day in the church organization should be dropped for the best good of society. If the reports are true it is no better or worse than it was with those filling high places in Bible times. It is folly to expect perfection in man or woman, and if a minister has erred, and has reformed, why not forgive instead of persecuting, especially when their doctrine should be forgive "seventy times seven," and charity for the erring. Has the minister ever been known to preach that a life he is accused of living as being right, or has he not on all occasions taught that the greater the purity, the higher the form of life? Are his accusers perfect in all things? Why destroy a man's usefulness and attempt to place him on a plane of life lower than he wants to live?

SPIRIT MATERIALIZATION is the last and most convincing phase of manifestation that has appeared; the entire public are being aroused to thought and action upon the subject. Was spirit materialization as recorded in the Bible a fact? Spirits are materializing themselves in different sections of the country; it is the same in all departments of human life, the true and the false exist. We can speak positively in saying that spirits do materialize themselves; that there are persons engaged in deceiving in this phase of manifestation is without question true; that there are those who possess genuine powers that deceive at times is also doubtless true.

What can be more convincing proof of immortality than to have spirits appear materialized, and as tangible to the material eye as though they were earth's inhabitants, precisely the same as they did more than eighteen hundred years ago, that is if history is correct. Hallucination, deception, or being psychologized is not applicable in all cases in speaking of this phase of manifestation.

While we were at Moravia a minister from Cape Cod was present, having been sent there by his society to investigate the genuineness of the manifestations; he was incog. to all present, not even giving his name, profession or residence; his son in spirit life, who was drowned, was there, appearing materialized, and gave the manner of his exit; also gave the family matters which convinced his parent, of the genuineness of the materialization. He returned to his home and society, with a full conviction of the reality of spirit materialization. He made this acknowledgment to his society, and in answer to the many letters received asking him if the accounts published in several papers were true as stated; he invariably replied in the following words "whereas I once believed in immortality I now know it to be true, as I have seen my son's spirit materialized and talked with him face to face."

Not long since a church member said to us that he thought one statement in the Bible proved materialization to be truthful, which was this: "As the disciples were sitting with closed doors, Jesus appeared [materialized] in their midst."

As these manifestations are becoming quite common it is more than useless to give long accounts of them;

one fact well authenticated is as good as a thousand. While we were at Chittenden there appeared many different spirits at each seance, which were recognized by relatives and friends. We will here state that it was a physical impossibility to arrange or place machinery so that what appeared to be spirits was deception; therefore we must come to the conclusion that what is seen at these seances are disembodied spirits materialized. There have been reliable, accredited accounts given of materialization in all the principal cities of the States, either in full size or faces and hands, which are not as convincing to skeptics as the spirit itself fully materialized, talking, singing and walking about.

For the past twenty five years spirits have materialized their hands through many different mediums; sometimes they would place them in smooth surface flour, leaving different sizes; recently William Denton has discovered a novel way of obtaining casts of spirit faces and hands in the presence of several different mediums, the spirits placing their hands in melted paraffine. Plaster casts are taken from these moulds. This is no more convincing than the spirit hand itself to the believer. Doubtless mediums who have had materialization either in the dark or light can obtain these moulds if they desire them.

Darkness is a condition requisite for obtaining spirit casts, while the spirits in full form are materialized and walk out into the light; darkness does not necessarily imply deception, but it causes suspicion with skeptics, who do not have absolute test conditions placed upon those engaged in obtaining materializations.

We doubt the propriety of holding advertised public paying seances for spirit manifestation until the medium is unfolded to the extent of giving manifestations that leaves the skeptic without doubt, as to their genuineness.

Doubtless much that appears which resembles our spirit friends is performed by familiar spirits, and is not in fact our spirit friends, only in representation. A well informed spirit who understands the spiritual law can without doubt materialize spirits of different sizes, also wearing apparel, jewelry or anything they desire. It is not reasonable to suppose that a young child has the power or ability to materialize itself. In this solution it may explain why the seeming mystery and conflicting testimony exists between different investigators.

The law of spirit transfer has been tested to the entire satisfaction of many close investigators: that which affects the spirit materialized body will affect the medium whose forces produce them; therefore caution should be exercised; there are reliable persons who testify that the material body of the medium has been fully spiritualized or dematerialized while the materializations are transpiring.

Such being the fact, the tying and untying of the medium, also placing iron rings upon the arms, taking off and putting on coats, is more in name than in reality; these things seem strange and incomprehensible and may be better understood in the future; there is at least a mystery hanging over these accredited manifestations.

We cannot see that it is possible for material substance to exist in the spirit world; the temporary materialization of a body for a spirit, is doubtless accomplished by the spirit attracting chemicals from the medium's organism and the surrounding elements which are contained in the atmosphere; it is the same with spirit flowers in their materialization. It has been proposed on seeing a materialized spirit to test its reality that a bullet should be fired through it; report says that it has been done, but we think none but those ignorant of the law of spirit materialization would attempt such an experiment. It is a well attested fact that a portion of the elements that make up the materialized body return to the medium on its being dematerialized; therefore what would affect the spirit body would affect the medium whose forces produced it.

If what has been stated be true, is it strange that some persons are afraid to meet the spirits gone before, especially those whom they have, while in earth life been guilty of deceiving and injuring? Some persons think that the "dead" know not anything, but spiritualism reveals the fact that spirits never were more alive and active than while in spirit life; this should be a warning to all who do not do right and deal justly. Spiritualism seems to be more feared at the present time than the doctrine of a future punishment in a "burning hell," and takes the place of a judgment, as the spirit inhabitants can and do reveal crime, hypocrisy, deception and vice. When persons approach the spiritually unfolded they are seen for their own worth and as they are.

SPIRIT PHOTOGRAPHY has been discussed pro and con as to the genuineness of the likenesses that appear upon the plates; most of the photographers who are not engaged in taking them pronounce the most that appear of mundane sphere production. We cannot doubt but what spirits can materialize and their likenesses be taken, but it is difficult to discover the genuine from those manufactured to order; there are as many different kinds taken as there are artists that take them; each artist's work has a universal appearance with all that they take, but do not look like those taken by any other artists: if genuine this may be accounted for by the quality of forces generated in the artist's organism. The differing of the likeness taken by the different artists either shows different processes of taking them, or that they originate in mundane spheres. If we were favored with such a gift we would not only prove to the world that they were honestly taken as claimed, but would call them spirit photographs at all times and places. The artists themselves must know for a certainty, whether genuine or manufactured to order. We are sorry that there are many things that look mysterious in this phase of spirit manifestations. The artists that are taking them have little or no confidence in any other artist's productions; this is a bad omen to say the least. We wish there was no chance for deception, as it would prove one of the most convincing proofs of the reality of spirit individuality for all mankind in the future life.

It has been suggested that four lenses be used by spirit artists in testing their reliability; in this way it would show readily whether made to order, or whether the spirit itself was actually present. If they were placed on the plate to order, they could not without much pains be placed in exact position upon each plate.

We can in part comprehend how a camera can take likenesses of materialized spirits, but cannot understand how the camera can discern objects that the material eye does not recognize. In taking spirit likenesses where there is no materialization, what can be the need of a camera? Why not prepare a plate for the picture and let the spirit do the rest, the same as they project their profiles upon window curtains, glass, etc. If the room is full of spirits, as is claimed by spirits themselves, and it is a fact that photographs of them are taken when not discerned by the material eye, why do they not appear in groups on the plates with any operator, while the camera is set at random?

The above criticism is only made for the artists (if any) who know that they are deceiving the public; the honest spirit artist will concur in this exposition.

INFIDELITY and *Infidels* are expressions that have been applied to believers in spirit communion in a reproachful manner. We think the words equally applicable to all persons who do not believe in modern spiritualism, or are in opposition to *our* belief, let it be what it may.

Often spiritualists show to skeptics and the world much inconsistency in their actions, and it would seem as though they were trying in all ways possible to destroy the effects of the knowledge obtained. Who ever heard of any other form of religious believers where its advocates did not work more in harmony and unison for the sustaining and promulgating their teachings! Individual interests, cliques, rings and selfish motives are too prominent to have united action; persons act out their own natures. Spiritualists do not seem interested in building up a church organization which does not include all humanity, and if they were they doubtless would be thwarted, as it does not seem to be their mission. They employ persons to speak for them who have no faith or belief in a future life beyond the change "death." The following are the words of one that has often been employed to speak for them:

"In his opinion spiritualism was a humbug, and many honest believers in it were gulled every day. He didn't believe in the immortality of the soul, and said that there was no proof of an after life. He didn't live next week and he didn't know that he would until next week arrived. He wasn't conscious of an existence before he was born, and couldn't be conscious of life after death until he had wound up his career on earth. He asked if the mediums of the day did not carry on their seances because "there was millions in it," and replied that he was informed by mediums that they gave " manifestations for the purpose of making money."

It is a mystery to us that intelligent infidels teach the philosophy and law of progression, and ignore spirit identity after death; also it seems strange and inconsistent for spiritualists to employ persons to speak for them who do not recognize individuality after the body is separated from the spirit.

Within a short time three noted Unitarian ministers have publicly stated that they did not know anything of human life beyond the gate called death; also a professor in one of the oldest colleges of this country, in a late lecture attempted to prove that there was to be a literal, material resurrection of the body, and that Jesus' body was materially raised, and gave proofs from the Bible for his belief. The entire evangelical churches combined teach that the material body is to be resurrected in the future; they know nothing of a future life except through the eye of faith, the Bible distinctly stating "the dead know not anything."

The Second Adventists (Miller as leader) mistook the new dispensation (spiritualism) for the end of the world, and as a whole, cannot see their error to this day. The Roman Catholics teach that spirits are active in "purgatory" and can progress out of it; at the same time warn their followers to flee from spiritualism, which is one and the same thing in reality, as far as the destiny of the spirit being fixed eternally on its entrance to spirit life. Spiritualists are the only class of individuals that actually preach with a knowledge of a future life for all mankind, suited to each person's growth, and which is continually changing, and progressive as aspirations and conditions will admit. This being the case should they not feel encouraged, and be willing to proclaim it in all of its diversified phases and conditions with truthfulness, and without fear or favor, looking only for the best interest of all mankind?

Capital Punishment is generally considered by spiritualists to be the relics of a barbarous age, therefore they are opposed to hanging (called capital punishment) as a means of correcting society, or as punishment and an example.

When a person takes the life of another individual, as a general thing they do it in an uncontrollable fit of anger, or in an excited state of mind, which is produced from various causes, or while the mind is unbalanced, (insane.) A nation hangs its victim while there is a cool deliberation entered into, doing it as is supposed, for the best good of society. Is the murderer or the nation the most to blame? This question must be solved in the future if not here. We think that persons born with evil tendencies and who are unsafe, should be confined for a material life if the case warrants it; the confinement should be for the protection of society; also that the crime may not be repeated. If the health of the criminal admits, they should be self-sustaining.

When it is realized that sending spirits to spirit life is no punishment, that the spirit after the execution is not dead but alive and active, and can do harm in one sphere of life as well as in the other, then will government adopt a new system of punishment that will educate the criminals and make them fit spirits to dwell in spirit life before sending them there.

REASONS WHY SPIRITUALISTS DO NOT ORGANIZE, AND THE ULTIMATE RESULT OF THEIR TEACHINGS.

Why spiritualists do not organize as do other religious denominations is often asked by the public. We will give our views of the mission of spiritualism, others may differ, which is or should be a part of the spiritual philosophy, "agree to disagree" on minor points. Belief does not change anything in nature; being lost or saved has nothing to do with the subject; our destiny is not so easily formed, and by saying I believe or disbelieve does not change the laws of life.

In many cases individuals must belong to some church or be wealthy to be recognized as suitable candidates for office; the ring and clique business should not be encouraged by spiritualists. Nothing short of an organization in religious belief, which includes all humanity can be lasting. Organization for government, protection and business purposes, which includes local ones for the promulgation of what individuals consider the truth is desirable and beneficial, but a national religious organization in a free country seems out of place. In selecting persons for office, capacity and integrity should be sought, in preference to showing favors to friends, who have not ability and qualifications; "loaves and fishes" should be secondary when adaptation and responsibility are required. The prospect for a sectarian spiritual organization is not as perceptible to-day, as it was ten years ago; many satisfactory reasons could be given for this state of things. We will not discuss them at this time as the facts must be evident to all who have investigated the subject to any extent. In our previous work entitled "An exposition of Spiritualism" we stated some of the reasons which seems sufficient, as the facts bear out the statements therein made; but as many spiritualists are not aware of the exertions that have been made by some of the leading spiritualists we will state a few facts for their benefit as well as the public.

The question should not be "Are you in favor of organization?" but "Does the spirit world, or the power that rules design that a fact of such importance to all mankind shall be acknowledged universally, or shall it be sectarian, as other forms of religious organizations that oppose it?" Why should those who accept spiritualism organize any more than those who believe in magnetism, chemistry and astronomy? Are not old religious organizations shaky, its members inharmonious, and are not such crumbling at their foundation, being false in theory? We cannot see that spiritualism is to be used as a power to war with other organizations, except it be by a slow, natural process of growth which undermines. There are local and national organizations for government and protection, which are the best that the people know as a whole. These change as people advance in growth, but this great truth must be universal. The means to be used in advancing the truth may be organized or not, as best suits the conditions and locality that persons are called to labor in. What other doctrine has advanced at such a rapid pace, and that too without any combined action or large money fund to draw from? Is not this a sure indication that spiritualism has a broader and larger field of action than a sectarian organization? That these statements are sustained by the facts themselves, we will give a brief history of the conventions that have been held; some attending, no doubt, for an honest purpose of helping the cause ; but the results thus far have proven unsuccessful, and shows that there is no limitation or bonds made by the crude elements of society that can blend all grades of persons into one sphere of thought and action. Time may develop conditions for a harmonious religious organization, but to us it does not seem to be the order of things, any more than it would be to harmonize evil with good. Both must work together to gain benefit, but not in any sense different from what all grades of society work together. Most spiritualists develop individuality and they assert their views with decided opinion. Some of them think this age far in advance of ancient times spoken of in history, and that progress marks the hour; but others think differently, and are attempting to produce manifestations said to have occurred in ages past; therefore their progress must be backward, the advocating of teachings that have gradually been buried in oblivion as civilization advances, seems unprofitable and more especially so for progressionists, that is without history is to repeat itself; therefore they cannot harmonize upon the issues of life, as do the willing subjects who take the opinions of others as their guide. The principal papers in this country devoted to the advancement of the spiritual philosophy do not harmonize in all issues that are claimed by some persons to be germane to spiritualism, but as they do not claim to be infallible, they no doubt are doing their work as best they can, each in its own sphere of usefulness, and acting from their highest convictions of right.

The first and last gatherings were mass conventions, the others were represented by delegates, in many cases self appointed, or made so by their presence. The first gathering being in Chicago ended in a division, politics crept in and caused it; the one held last year in Boston proved to be the last and must be resuscitated under different auspices, that is if it is to be known as a spiritualistic movement. Most spiritualists look upon organization thus far as a farce and take no interest either in conventions or an organization; consider them useless appendages.

In the last call made, the names of "Spiritualism, Free Religion, and Infidels" were made use of for the purpose of discussing the subject of "Social Freedom," the affair being run almost exclusively by a few freedomites, the local papers honestly called it by its right name, "a Free Love Convention." The above names doubtless were used without consent or approval, and as a cloak to gain a respectable hearing; it being a socialistic gathering almost exclusively. There was but one side represented, they could have voted any person into office or any resolution into existence if they had been called upon to vote; without doubt a few of the wise ones saw that it would not answer to show their strength, therefore voted it inexpedient to vote upon the resolutions under consideration; this act prevented the united action from being known to the public, and to-day it is not known whether the different societies named in the call approved or disapproved of the proceedings.

We will copy extracts from a letter published in the Index, Oct. 15 from a prominent radical, rational spiritualist, which states the facts in brief. He said "It could with as much propriety be called a cattle show as a spiritual convention, and it is this fact that leads me to write this letter. There was but a very slight sprinkling of Boston spiritualists present; many of these like myself were present from curiosity rather than interest. The subject of spiritualism was entirely left out." He also styled it a ship sailing under false colors, and that when he was in Parker Memorial Hall on the 17th of September he was not in a spiritualists' convention and it was an offense to a good many spiritualists to call it one.

The Philadelphia convention desired to make the organization perpetual, all but five voting for it; delegates were to become life members. We were one of the five that voted against its being continued in that form, and the results to-day show how impractical it would have been. The Troy convention proved to be a great farce on a small scale; rings, cliques were the order and were so thin that it seemed a mystery how intelligent individuals could be drawn into it. There was in fact no president chosen at this convention; the second ballot there was ninety votes cast all told, three candidates for the office; two of them had forty two votes each, the other six votes.

The enthusiasm and large promises of funds to carry on the work was proclaimed as fitness for the office. Pamphlets and books were distributed according to the influence each delegate possessed, varying in price from forty cents to three dollars; each speaker having a set of books, the rest of the delegates having her biography by Theodore Tilton etc., the presents creating a sort of sympathy; the life of such a wonderful woman made the psychological effect more catching and the work after this was easily accomplished. One of the delegates asked the candidate this question, "If you are elected as president, will it be detrimental to your prospects of being elected to the presidency of the United States?" The candidate with tears coursing down her cheeks, knew just how to reach and affect the sympathetic audience, replied that she did not care if it did, etc. This was enough to finish the work. Some of the delegates did not seem to think that there was anything more to be done in the way of labor in the cause, others declared that fifty thousand dollars was to be given to the cause the next year if the candidate was elected. We looked on with amazement at the proceedings, and could not help thinking what excitement and foolishness; persons who had labored faithfully for fifteen years as lecturers did not get a chance to be heard during the convention, while the nominated candidate (from her own statement) acknowledged that she never entered a spiritual convention previous, was allowed the principal part of two evenings, as well as much of the time during one day session.

It was afterwards announced that she was elected president of the association. We never desire to see such a farce played by a body of spiritualists again, it being their doctrine to discountenance anything that borders upon the ring and clique business in others. We had this only solution as explanation, which was that the angel world was wiser than mortals, and blinded some of the delegates to the conditions and facts, and made use of the available element for the purpose of destroying the last vestige of the national organization which was successfully accomplished, and from that day to this almost the entire interest at the gatherings has been confined to "social freedom."

Spiritualists to-day have no national organization, neither have they but few working local ones, and the reasons are evident to all who take a comprehensive view of the entire subject.

Stirpiculture or selection is a subject that was discussed at the last gathering. This subject is common with stock raising. Draught and carriage horses are more useful than the race or fast horse, but are not considered so valuable; all of them fill their sphere of usefulness, but we cannot with propriety compare the raising of human beings to that of the lower animals, as all individuals have certain rights that cannot with consistency be taken from them by delegated popes.

It seems well that individuals are not organized alike or think alike, and are not equal in mentality. Different developments can be made available in their own sphere of life; finite beings cannot make the universal standard for all society; individuals seem to be fitted for all branches of labor and usefulness and to all grades of life, mentally, physically and spiritually; different individuals should seek to find their own natural adaptation. Society must advance as a whole and while there is a demand for the coarser material work, there must be those fitted to accomplish it, and the pope style of making selections would not improve society as a whole or aid progression as we see it.

There is no perfection with the human; knowledge never changes; all persons' beliefs are liable to change, therefore the public should look upon the various opinions and actions connected with spiritualists, as they do upon the actions and beliefs of society in general under other names, no better or worse, without there is something to warrant it. Mankind cannot change the laws of the universe; ignorance and undeveloped actions are prominent with the various societies and people. By taking this view more harmony will be developed, and the subject be better understood. Truth and justice must come uppermost in the end, therefore it is better to wait patiently for the growth. Human beings exist to-day fitted for all kinds of labor; what some lack in spiritual, others do in their material; which has the prefference while dwelling in mundane spheres is a question not easily solved by mankind. Are not all grades of society essential to assist the designs of the infinite? Why could not the human race have been made perfect if such was the intention, thereby saving a continual struggling to reach a higher and more perfect growth?

If spiritualists formed organizations which only included their own belief, what better would they be than those they are not in harmony with in that direction? Sectarian organizations cannot be permanent, as they conflict with the natural order of things. There are so many shades of opinions with the spiritualists that it is impossible to bind them together except as all society is bound. Without doubt spiritualism is the leaven in society and cannot be confined or limited, therefore its mission is not to form permanent organizations outside of all society. As proofs of these statements we will say that there are a number of trance mediums settled over other religious denominations, and daily we hear of ministers that have outgrown their previous religious teachings, and have become converted or convinced of the truthfulness of spiritualism, and are willing to preach it, thus showing that its mission is to work in and through all society, and to know no bounds or limits outside of the entire whole.

In dealing with this subject we have endeavored to take law and principle instead of speculative theories, knowing that which harmonizes with the past must of necessity continue on in the future. It may be falsely interpreted in this solution as conveying the idea that the "all right doctrine" is correct.

We cannot see all things as far as human beings' actions are concerned, to be all right; all things exist as they are subject to continual change; if all things were right it would destroy the need of progression. We can conceive of all things being wrong to-day, but in the tomorrow may be righted; cause and effect exist and the playing upon words does not make wrong right, and often leads the ignorant to do unbecoming things, planting themselves upon the all right doctrine as an excuse for wrong doing. If persons would abstain from doing what they know to be *wrong* and would do what they know to be *right*, there would be much suffering prevented, not only for themselves but others.

Great ignorance abounds concerning what spiritualism is and what it is not, and how it affects the lives of individuals is not generally understood. If the natural life forces were better understood by mankind, there would be less selfishness, war and bloodshed; the acts of life would become more natural instead of being superficial; and knowledge would supersede ignorance. Human laws will be needed just as long as selfishness exists; arbitration is better than going to law to settle disputes, but as there are so many persons that seem to care nothing for their word or honor that it is almost impossible to settle some just claims except by disinterested jurors.

We could relate several cases that have come under our own personal knowledge that would warrant the extreme penalty of the law, but as such cases are common with all individuals who are dealing with society in a business point, we will refrain to publish them even if our desire is almost uncontrollable to show the injustice and rascality that has been practised upon us personally, and that too by persons who have held high positions of trust, and others who are moving in good society. They must suffer most in the end, and that is our only consolation.

RULES AND CONDITIONS beneficial to individuals having besetting vices or habits. Say "I will abandon them;" once said with a will and determination, the work is accomplished. Self harmony, self sustaining, self reliant, self respect, self company are conditions to be cultivated, which will lead to happiness.

In these times of crime and recklessness, extravagance and lack of morality, spiritualists should set an example by practising economy and living a life of stability.

Some persons advocate the necessity of all persons passing through low conditions to obtain higher ones; we think this injurious in its tendency and untrue in fact. If persons are low in their natures, they will remain so until they outgrow or overcome and subdue the lower. It is not necessary for persons to indulge in vice and ruinous habits to know of their effects. Is not the reason of man superior to the instinct of animals? Does not the animal often show greater wisdom than the human, that is in eating and drinking what the system requires and is beneficial?

In conclusion we will say that we are confident that what we said in our previous works will accord in harmony with our present views, thereby avoiding conflicting with previous statements. We can add to our knowledge, but it does not answer for us to vacillate and place on record statements to-day that have to be contradicted tomorrow. To gain confidence with the public it is better not to make statements without they can be first positively demonstrated; we can speculate upon things, but making assertions that we cannot prove is not wisdom or advisable.

Spiritualism better explains and harmonizes to the finite mind all things in life, and traces effects from causes, making all that exists in life "one great stupendous whole," than any other theory ever advanced. Sincerely do we believe that the seeming mysteries, imperfections connected with ancient spiritualism (as history records) is no more or less complicated or incomprehensible than is modern spiritualism in its manifestations. Both are beyond the full comprehension of the finite mind.

The European spiritual literature, with few exceptions, harmonizes with that which has been written in this country; thus showing that the various manifestations, laws and conditions are universal.

Spirit manifestations are high or low, as the spirits in and out of the material body attract to them, by and through their chemical forces, the manifestation depending entirely upon the controlling spirit, the medium and the investigator. We should not ignore the crude, undeveloped conditions of life, as they exist whether we desire them or not. Without doubt spirits on the lower plane of life are more detrimental to society than beneficial, and in some cases it would have been better if they had never been born. Spiritualism on the lower strata of human life is looked upon by some persons as being unworthy of their notice. Such persons are blind to the true state of life as it exists, and only see from their stand-point of development. Much misunderstanding exists by calling the same things by different names; for instance the undeveloped spirits are called "evil spirits," "diakka," lying spirits;" and now comes a new name, that of "elementary spirits," which has never been explained. Whether they are lower in the scale of existence than the vegetable cabbage or above the woodchuck, has not yet been made known to the public.

Spiritualists differ on many issues connected with human life, as do the church members in their non-essentials; there are many obstacles to overcome, but the philosophy being founded on facts, and infinite, immutable laws, it will eventually overcome crudities and imperfections: knowledge will take the place of belief, and of a necessity there must be in the future an acknowledgement by all mankind that spiritualism is a verity; its ultimate will develop the universal religious organization which will include all humanity.

Spiritualism when properly understood and realized harmonizes earth and spirit spheres, and also explains the subtle laws and philosophy of life, health and happiness.

VITAL MAGNETIC CURE.

AN EXPOSITION OF VITAL MAGNETISM;

AND ITS APPLICATION TO THE TREATMENT OF MENTAL AND PHYSICAL DISEASE.

BY A MAGNETIC PHYSICIAN.

"A more useful book for the student or family can not well be found. It is selling well, and gives satisfaction. It is a work that will not lose its interest in an age." — *Banner of Light.*

"There can be no doubt of the general and eager interest everywhere manifest in the infant science of vital magnetism. No skepticism opposes the facts slowly brought foward concerning it. Gratifying as the book is in both manner and matter, its glimpses and hints do scarcely more than whet the spirit of inquiry to know more." — *Woman's Journal.*

"I am much pleased with it; consider it a very useful book, and one that the public need." — *Mrs. Caroline Cobb.*

"This book deals with a subject that will grow strongly in favor when rightly presented, since the tendency is to the disuse of medicines, so far as can be, in the treatment of disease." — *South Boston Inquirer.*

"This is an interesting book, and contains useful hints in regard to health and sickness, so far as they refer to human beings and human agencies." — *Boston Investigator.*

"It contains much valuable information for the general reader." — *Am. Spiritualist.*

"Its high moral tone must be an additional recommendation of the work. That the human magnetic force, when properly understood and applied, is a powerful curative agent, especially in all nervous complaints, is now too well established to be denied; and the writer of 'Vital Magnetic Cure,' by an array of facts in his experience and that of others, has greatly helped to strengthen, if not to settle, the fact of its utility both for the preservation of health and the removal of disease." — *David Plumb.*

"A very valuable work, entitled as above, which deserves to be widely read, if not for the stand taken by the author in favor of a somewhat questionable remedial agent, certainly, however, for the many suggestions he throws out respecting the preservation of health. The time will come when it will be better known; and we therefore commend just such books as the one now spoken of, because they will at least familiarize people with that thing which will some day be better understood." — *Milford Journal.*

"I have read during the last ten years nearly every thing published on the application of magnetism to the cure of disease; and I deem this work an important addition to the literature of the subject, and of great practical value to every one who would learn how to successfully use this most efficient sanitive agency." — *W. F. Evans, M.D.*, Author of Mental Cure.

First edition exhausted in a few weeks.

For sale by COLBY & RICH.   PRICE $1,50.   Postage 20 cts.

NATURE'S LAWS IN HUMAN LIFE.

AN EXPOSITION OF SPIRITUALISM;

EMBRACING THE VARIOUS OPINIONS OF EXTREMISTS, PRO AND CON, TOGETHER WITH THE AUTHOR'S EXPERIENCE.

BY THE AUTHOR OF "VITAL MAGNETIC CURE."

As the title indicates, it takes a comprehensive view of the subject treated of. Opposing opinions are brought together side by side, and can be weighed in the balance. This mode of comparison practically puts Spiritualism on trial, and enables the reader to judge of its real merits. The absurdity of extreme views, born of prejudice rather than knowledge, is exposed. A mass of evidence is given in the form of narrative, which, for variety can not be found in any one publication. The interest awakened in Spiritualism is now world-wide; and it must, as alleged by its enemies, be a stupendous delusion or fraud, or of satanic origin, or, as claimed by its believers, a revolution of facts which brings one of the greatest blessings vouchsafed to mankind. The arguments are cogent, and presented in a spirited manner.

There are also miscellaneous subjects both of a practical and speculative nature discussed, which have grown out of the main subject, such as Marriage, Divorce, Free Love, Re-incarnation, a Criticism upon the Numerous Religious Organizations, &c. About 300 pp. Price $1.50. Postage 20 cts.

"Nature's Laws in Human Life."

Notices.

"It is an exhaustive summary of the best things, best persons, and best sayings, that have appeared in the great spiritual movement." — *Western Star.*

"Its real purpose is to place before the reader the facts and phenomena of what is called Spiritualism, and, in doing so, gives a pretty impartial statement of the different views respecting the asserted spiritual manifestations. He quotes from those who treat the whole matter as a deception, the mediums as jugglers, and their doings as a new phase of legerdemain. He gives the views of those like Elder Knapp, who admit the phenomena as of spiritual origin, but attribute them all to the cunning and power of the Devil. He quotes from those who occupy the scientific standpoint, and refer the phenomena to some not yet understood laws of mind and matter, to the exclusion of the *spirit* theory.

"On the affirmative side, — that *spirits* work the results, — the author thinks he finds much proof in the Bible and in the strange experience of Swedenborg. The book is, of course, for the most part, made up of the wonderful things done through the mediums, which he claims there is no accounting for in reason, except as being by spirit agency. The favorable opinion of great names is given to corroborate that view; and the reader is left to judge for himself, and decide as the proof may seem to demand.

"There is so much in this question of Spiritualism that cannot be scouted, but demands honest and earnest inquiry, that a book so full and so impartial on the subject as the one under consideration is entitled to be cordially received and widely read." — DAVID PLUMB.

"This work is principally a compilation of facts both for and against the philosophy of Spiritualism; and such has been the author's regard for the whole unvarnished truth, that we find nothing distorted or misrepresented on either side, but an array of facts, so detailed as to form a very readable and attractive book, such as all hesitating minds might peruse with profit." — *American Spiritualist.*

New Publications.

"We are at a loss to say which is the more interesting, — the testimony adduced by the author *pro* and *con*, or his own comments and discussions." — *Banner of Light.*

"Nature's Laws in Human Life."

"The work is written in a spirit of candor which commends itself to the reader. The author evidently has a sincere faith in the truth of Spiritualism. The *opinions* of its opponents are fairly stated, with no attempt to soften them down, and are answered by a record of facts drawn from the writer's large experience and extensive observation, and the principles fairly deducible from those facts. It is written in a clear and compact style, and is free from all offensive attacks upon other forms of religious belief. To the myriads of people in our land who long to know something about the reality of another life, and of communication with the unseen realm, and of the laws that govern it, this will be found a useful volume." — W. F. EVANS, author of "Mental Cure."

"The R. P. Journal," "Utica Herald," and many of the local papers, give long reviews of the book; and there is yet to be any thing said which would convey the idea that *prejudice* was shown on *either side of the subject*; but a candid statements of facts is shown, and the reader can decide the question. The book should interest the entire human family.

THE MENTAL CURE.

ILLUSTRATING THE INFLUENCE OF THE MIND ON THE BODY, BOTH IN HEALTH AND DISEASE,

AND THE PSYCHOLOGICAL METHOD OF TREATMENT.

By REV. W. F. EVANS.

THIS book has created a lively interest, not only among Spiritualists, but in the minds of members of the medical profession, and among persons of various religious denominations. It is an able treatise, and should be in the library of every thinking person, sick or well. It has received the encomiums of able critics. A reviewer in "The Banner of Light" says, —

"For originality of thought and treatment, for a certain intrepid directness which is the chief merit of a treatise of this character, and for a plain practicalness that commends its broad and profound truths, together with its more acute and intricate speculations, to the general readers, we think this volume will take its place at once among the remarkable productions of the day, and vindicate its reputation by the marked revolution it will set on foot in reference to common life and thinking.

"Along with this discussion, he sets forth the mode of regulating the intellectual and affectional nature of the invalid, under any system of medical treatment."

This is one of the best books we have on our shelves. — *R. P. Journal.*

Table of contents annexed. About 1,500 copies of first edition sold. A second edition to be issued soon. 364 pp. For sale by

COLBY & RICH,
9 MONTGOMERY PLACE, Boston, Mass.
Price $1.50. Postage 20 cents.

"MENTAL CURE."

Additional Testimonials.

"The power of mind over matter is discussed in a manner both interesting and suggestive. We commend it as presenting many truths worthy of attention." — *Woman's Journal.*

"Persons of a metaphysical turn of mind will find it interesting to study." — *South Boston Inquirer.*

H. A. Burbank writes of it thus: "The reader will find himself in the profound depths of the science of human nature, and wondering at the great simplicity, yet far-reaching relations, of the mysteries of life, mind, and spirit, when set forth by a mind fitted to *discern spiritual things*, and intuitively endued with the logical method to set them forth to another in a complete and rational system, and in the beautiful language of demonstrable truth."

A. E. Newton says, "It includes a knowledge of spiritual laws and forces which are intimately related to the welfare, the daily needs, physical and spiritual, of humanity in this life, as well as in that which is to come."

H. K. Hunt, M.D., after a practice of thirty years, says that "it should take the same place that 'Combe's Constitution of Man' did in its day, and become a standard work, and be sold by the ten thousands."

L. W. Abell, M.D., after twelve years' practice, speaks thus, "It is an invaluable book, and should be in every family."

Dr. A. Johnson, New York, says, "I have no hesitation in saying that it contains more sound philosophy in regard to the laws of life and health than all the medical works in the library."

"The Western Star," "Journal of Health," and "Phrenological Journal," speak in high appreciation of its merits; also Emma Hardinge-Britten, Lizzie Doten, A. J. Davis, Thomas Gales Forster, Giles B. Stebbins, authors and lecturers, commend it as being alive to the needs of this age.

www.ingramcontent.com/pod-product-compliance
Lightning Source LLC
Chambersburg PA
CBHW021918180426
43199CB00032B/708